How to Use
THE INTERNET

THIRD EDITION

How to Use

THE INTERNET

THIRD EDITION

HEIDI STEELE

Ziff-Davis Press
An imprint of Macmillan Computer Publishing USA
Emeryville, California

Acquisitions Editor	Suzanne Anthony
Copy Editor	Deborah Craig
Technical Reviewer	Doug Urner
Project Coordinator	Madhu Prasher
Proofreader	Jeff Barash
Book Design	Dennis Gallagher/Visual Strategies, San Francisco
Technical Illustration	Sarah Ishida
Word Processing	Howard Blechman
Page Layout	Janet Piercy
Indexer	Julie Kawabata

Ziff-Davis Press, ZD Press, and the Ziff-Davis Press logo are trademarks or registered trademarks of, and are licensed to Macmillan Computer Publishing USA by Ziff-Davis Publishing Company, New York, New York.

Ziff-Davis Press imprint books are produced on a Macintosh computer system with the following applications: FrameMaker®, Microsoft® Word, Quark Xpress®, Adobe Illustrator®, Adobe Photoshop®, Adobe Streamline™, MacLink® *Plus,* Aldus® FreeHand™, and Collage Plus™.

Ziff-Davis Press, an imprint of
Macmillan Computer Publishing USA
5903 Christie Avenue
Emeryville, CA 94608

ISBN 1-56276-450-0
Manufactured in the United States of America
10 9 8 7 6 5 4

TABLE OF CONTENTS

ACKNOWLEDGMENTS

As this project comes to a close, I have the happy task of thanking the many people who contributed to the book.

I'm grateful to Cheryl Applewood and Suzanne Anthony for getting this project underway, and for giving me an excuse to putter on the Internet for hours on end and call it work.

It was truly a joy to work with all the members of my "dream team." Deborah Craig, a superb author herself, was gracious enough to do the copy edit. She gave expert advice born of years of experience, also sprinkling the manuscript with plenty of humorous Post-Its to keep my spirits from flagging. The technical reviewer, Doug Urner, brought a tremendous amount of Internet know-how and good cheer to the project. He also raised the concept of multitasking to a new level: Never before have I met someone who could simultaneously revise HTML code, send e-mail, discuss the finer points of Web security, and joke about poodles during a 2:00 a.m. brainstorming session. I'm delighted to have received his valuable input on this project.

Madhu Prasher, project editor, was a pleasure to work with, both because she handled the project so adeptly and because she insisted on visiting my dog each time I dropped by the press. Thanks to Kelly Green, development editor extraordinaire, for getting the project off the ground, and to Kim Haglund for taking over when Kelly went on tour with her band. (A talented bunch, these Ziff-Davis folks!) Thanks also to Sarah Ishida for the art work, to Janet Piercy for the page layout, and to Howard Blechman for the word processing. I'm grateful to William Sommers at Televolve and to Duane Fields and Jessica James at Netscape for deftly answering a barrage of questions about ISPs and browsers.

Finally, I'd like to thank Chad Foutz for his many knowledgeable comments and suggestions, and for generously lending his computer when the need arose, and Thea Noelle Steele, my most favorite niece, for contributing to the chapters on Web design.

INTRODUCTION

 Countless people now use the Internet, and there are probably almost as many reasons for wanting to learn about it. Whether you want to research a subject online; decipher your child's "cyber chatter" about URLs, ISPs, and FTP; or just find out what the hoopla is all about, *How to Use the Internet* will give you the skills you need to integrate the Internet into your life. You will learn about a broad range of topics—how to set up an Internet connection at home, browse the World Wide Web, download software, send e-mail, and even create your own Web site.

This book assumes that you're using (or plan on using) Netscape Navigator 3.0 on a Windows 95 computer. (Netscape Navigator—often simply called *Netscape*—is a browser program. Although browsers are primarily designed to access the World Wide Web, you can use them to access other parts of the Internet as well.) However, the focus of the book is not on the specific software you're using to access the Internet, but on the Internet itself. Because all browsers have similar capabilities, you can benefit from reading this book even if you are using another browser, such as Microsoft's Internet Explorer.

The resources available on the Internet are changing and expanding so rapidly that trying to describe them is as challenging as getting a litter of wriggling puppies to stay still long enough for a group photograph. Given this state of affairs, the best approach to learning about the Internet is not to depend on a "yellow pages" type directory of resources (resources come and go on a daily basis) but rather, to focus on the tools you need to explore the Internet. If you get a good handle on these tools, you can use them to find out about new resources on your own and keep abreast of changes on the Internet as they occur.

The chapters in this book contain a series of related topics that span two facing pages. In other words, everything you need to know about a subject is in front of you at one time. Each two-page spread is arranged in a series of numbered steps that revolve around a central graphic image, which reinforces the concepts at hand.

"Tip Sheets" in each topic also provide valuable shortcuts, additional explanations, and otherwise edifying material. In addition, you'll find three "Try It!" sections at strategic spots in this book. A Try It! is a hands-on exercise that lets you practice the skills you've acquired so far. As you read these sections, be sure to follow each step at your computer.

Finally, the intent of this book is not to encourage you to use the Internet for its own sake. Contrary to some reports, the Internet is not a panacea for all your ills: It won't take the gray out of your hair or make your child like spinach. Nonetheless, the Internet can enrich your life in some wonderful and probably unexpected ways. Your mission, should you choose to accept it, is to discover the specific constellation of Internet resources that works for you.

CHAPTER 1

The Internet: A Global Resource

The Internet is fast becoming an integral part of our personal and professional lives. Through the Internet, you can stay in touch with a close friend living abroad, trade stocks, watch movie clips, do research, or take orders from customers. What makes the Internet so exciting is that it can mean such different things to different people. It is an all-purpose tool that you can shape to fit the contours of your own lifestyle, work, and interests.

This chapter will help you get your bearings in this new landscape before venturing off to explore its nooks and crannies. The chapter starts with some examples of what you can do on the Internet—this should get you thinking about what parts you'd most like to explore. Next, you'll learn a little about the origins of the Internet and how it's put together.

Finally, an overview of the Internet would not be complete without an introduction to the World Wide Web. The Web provides a graphical interface to the Internet and integrates multimedia into online documents. The Web is not only the means by which most people access the Internet, it also represents the cutting edge of Internet development. For these reasons, it's important to incorporate the Web into your view of the Internet from the very beginning.

What Can I Do on the Internet?

The possibilities on the Internet are truly endless. New resources sprout up daily, so if you keep an eye out, you will continue discovering things that pique your interest. All the resources mentioned here are discussed in greater depth in later chapters, so for now, just take note of the ones that strike your fancy.

TIP SHEET

▶ The terms *Web site* and *home page* refer to a collection of documents on the World Wide Web. You'll learn much more about Web sites in "What Is the World Wide Web?" later in this chapter.

▶ The cryptic strings of characters on this page that begin with *http://* are called URLs (for *uniform resource locators*); they are the addresses you use to access resources on the Internet. You'll learn how URLs are constructed in the next chapter.

▶ Don't worry if you don't yet have a way to connect to the Internet and the World Wide Web. You'll learn how to get set up in Chapters 3 and 4.

▶ When you think of a topic you'd like to explore, jot it down. That way, when you start poking around the Internet, you'll have some specific subjects to investigate. Otherwise, you can easily spend hours on the Internet without anything to show for it—kind of like wandering around Price Club or WalMart without a shopping list.

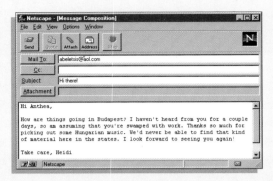

1 E-mail (electronic mail) lets you type messages and send them via the Internet to people around the globe for the price of a local phone call. Using e-mail, you can collaborate on projects or keep a daily banter going with a friend in another country. E-mail also allows you to include files—word processing documents, spreadsheets, and so on—along with your messages.

8 You can design your own Web site. Don't be intimidated by all the flashy sites set up by the big corporations. One of the beauties of the Internet is that there is still plenty of room

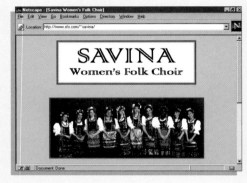

for the "little guy," and as with the rest of life, simpler is often better. This example shows the site for my choir (http://www.sfo.com/~savina).

7 You can, of course, shop 'til you drop on the Internet. Online "malls" give you a virtual shopping basket and let you walk the aisles. After you pay at the checkout, the company ships the products to you via postal mail. The site shown here is a virtual CD store (http://www.cdworld.com).

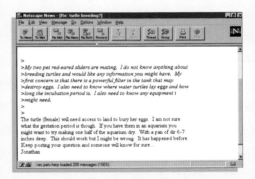

2 The Internet lets you "travel" all over the world. Here is the Web site for Peking University in China (http://www.pku.edu.cn). You can also visit museums such as the Louvre in Paris (http://www.mistral. culture.fr/louvre) or gather information for an upcoming overseas vacation by hopping over to local sites in the countries of interest.

3 You can choose among literally thousands of different software programs available on the Internet, many of which are free. When you find one you want to try, just download it and then install it on your computer. The Web site shown here (http://www.tucows.com) provides links to a wide variety of programs.

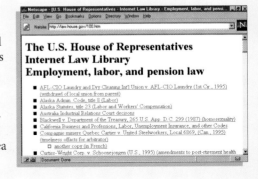

4 If you have a hobby, no matter how obscure, a group of people with the same interest undoubtedly share information over the Internet in *newsgroups* or *mailing lists*. The example here shows an exchange in a discussion group for people who share a penchant for reptilian and amphibian pets.

6 Most public institutions have an online presence. You may find yourself visiting some of these sites regularly to get up-to-date information. Shown here is one of my favorites, the Web site for National Public Radio (http://www.npr.org). *Not* shown here is one of my least favorites, the IRS (http://www.irs.ustreas.gov/prod).

5 The Internet is an ideal place to conduct research. Libraries around the world have resources available online. There are also many privately managed collections of online reference materials. This example shows the employment law area of the Internet Law Library, which is maintained by the U.S. House of Representatives (http://law.house.gov).

What Is the Internet?

The Internet is a global collection of interconnected computer networks. The easiest way to understand it is to start by looking at small-scale networks, and then build up step by step to a picture of the Internet in its entirety.

▶ **1** A *network* is simply a bunch of computers that are connected (via cables, phone lines, high-speed data lines, or satellite) so that they can share resources and information.

TIP SHEET

▶ **No single entity controls the Internet. Rather, individual components of it are managed by various public and private institutions. Many Internet old-timers are deeply committed to the notion that the Internet should remain a decentralized, slightly anarchistic place that welcomes the free exchange of ideas.**

▶ **Private networks aren't automatically a part of the Internet; they have to decide to connect, and this often requires special hardware and software, as described in the next chapter under "How Does the Internet Work?"**

▶ **The Internet is much more than the sum of its parts; it also encompasses the incredible wealth of resources that are stored on Internet computers, as well as the contributions of millions of people who maintain and add to those resources.**

7 In the "old days," it was hard to view anything but text-based documents on the Internet. That changed with the advent of the World Wide Web, because Web documents can include colors, graphic images, sound and video clips, animation, and more. (There are still many valuable text-based resources on the Internet, however, and you'll learn how to use them in Chapters 10 through 15.) Pictured here are text-based and graphical views of the Library of Congress.

Text-based view

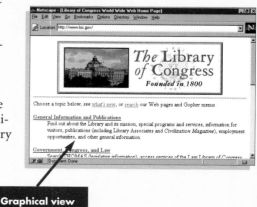

Graphical view

2 The term *local area network* (LAN) describes interconnected computers—all fairly close to one another—that not only share hardware resources such as printers but also share software and data. A small company may have all its computers connected in one LAN; large companies may have a separate LAN for each department, and may then cable the LANs together to form a larger LAN.

3 In many LANs, there is at least one computer (normally a very fast one with a lot of disk space) designated as the *file server*. The other computers on the network can electronically access both programs and data stored on the file server. This allows people to share files without having to distribute them in printed form or on floppy disks. LANs also let people send e-mail to other people on the network and perform many other collaborative tasks.

4 Large businesses and organizations use high-speed data lines to connect LANs in separate geographical locations so that the staff in all their offices can communicate and share resources. This type of setup is called a *wide area network* (WAN). By using satellites or fiber-optic cables, WANs can even connect offices located on different continents.

5 The Internet is a motley but effective assortment of large-scale WANs run by private companies (mostly long distance phone companies such as AT&T, Sprint, and MCI). This "backbone" connects all manner of private, commercial, government, and academic networks, as well as a growing number of home computers.

6 In its early years (the 1970s and 1980s), the Internet was used primarily by academics, scientists, and military personnel as a way of sharing work-related information and collaborating on projects. But scientists soon started using the Internet to share favorite recipes and gossip, and news of this new form of communication quickly spread to nontechnical people and companies around the world.

What Is the World Wide Web?

The World Wide Web is a vast collection of documents stored on Internet computers. Two things make Web documents (usually called *Web pages*) special. First, they contain *links* (either pictures or words you can click on) that lead to other Web pages. Second, they can contain graphics, sound, and other multimedia elements, which opens up many new possibilities for presenting information. The Web is technically only one part of the Internet, but it has become so popular that many new Internet users believe the Web *is* the Internet.

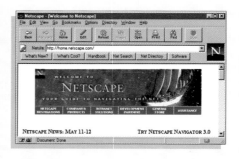

TIP SHEET

▶ **The relationship between browsers and Web servers is called a *client/server* relationship. The client (in this case your browser) requests information from the server (in this case the Web server containing the requested Web page) and the server delivers it.**

▶ **A Web server can support one Web site or many different sites. A Web site can also be so large that several computers are needed to handle all the requests from browsers.**

▶ **Security is an important issue with interactive Web sites, because there is a risk that information you enter in on-line forms, such as your credit card number or your travel plans, could be intercepted by a "cyberthief." For this reason, many companies are now developing "secure" Web sites that use cryptography to ensure that sensitive information doesn't fall into the wrong hands. See Chapter 15 for the details about security on the Web.**

▶ **1** Computers that store Web pages are called *Web servers*. There is nothing special about these computers, except that they have a full-time connection to the Internet and they run Web server software. You access pages on Web servers by using a program called a *browser*. As soon as you tell your browser what Web page you want to view, it goes to the Web server that holds the page and retrieves it for you. Here is Netscape Navigator, one of the most widely used browsers.

A simple yet effective page

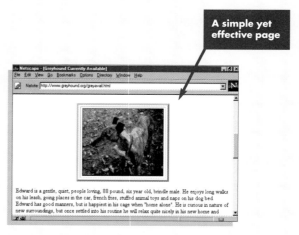

 Even though some Web sites have lots of bells and whistles, there is absolutely nothing wrong with simple Web pages that just include text and graphics. This page is from a greyhound rescue organization. One of the best things about Web pages is that they are easy to create and inexpensive to "publish." Chapters 17 through 21 teach you how to get your own Web site up and running.

Links to other Web sites

2 The links contained in Web pages can point to areas within the same page, to other pages residing on the same Web server, or to pages sitting on some computer on the other side of the world.

3 The term *Web site* refers to a collection of one or more Web pages created by one person, company, or organization on the Web. At its simplest, a Web site can consist of just one page, but the Web sites of major companies normally contain dozens or even hundreds of individual Web pages, all linked together.

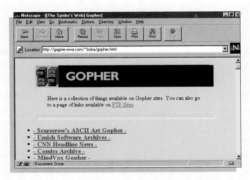

4 Web pages can also contain links to resources on the Internet that predate the Web, such as FTP and gopher sites. This fact makes the Web an ideal jumping off point for exploring the Internet, because it gives you access to all the things the Internet has to offer.

A colorful and technically sophisticated page

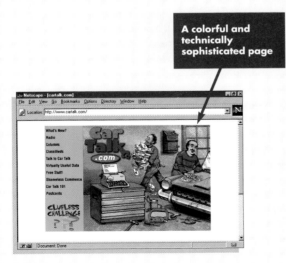

6 Web sites have grown quite sophisticated. As you'll soon discover, it isn't uncommon to find Web sites that include sound, animation, and video.

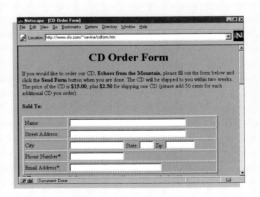

5 Web pages are becoming increasingly interactive. For example, instead of merely presenting information or graphics for you to view, many sites also include online forms that you fill in and send back to the owner of the site. These forms are useful for letting customers order products or fill in questionnaires. This example is a simple order form for my choir's CD.

CHAPTER 2

Understanding the Internet

As when learning about other new technologies, you can take a couple of equally valid approaches to learning about the Internet. The first is simply to learn enough to do what you need to do on the Internet. This technique is typified by the statement, "I don't care how it *works*; just tell me how to *use* it." The second approach is to "peek under the hood" and learn a bit about the inner workings of the Internet before taking the leap into cyberspace. People who like this type of approach generally say things like, "I have to understand what makes it tick before I can try it out."

If learning the finer points of data communication doesn't make you jump for joy, and if you already have an Internet account that includes Web access, feel free to skip this chapter for now. If, however, you're either congenitally curious or you have to set up Internet access yourself, you'll probably find this material worthwhile.

First, you'll learn how information is transmitted across the Internet and what types of hardware and software are required for Internet access. Next, you'll discover what technologies are working behind the scenes to make the World Wide Web worthy of the current fanfare. Finally, you'll find out what e-mail addresses and URLs (uniform resource locators) are and how they are constructed. This knowledge should make them easier to guess if you lose that little scrap of paper on which you jotted one down.

How Does the Internet Work?

One of the reasons the Internet works so well is that all types of computers—UNIX-based machines, PCs, Macs, and so on—can connect to it and share information. This is possible because there are technical standards that describe how all the computers on the Internet talk to each other.

▶ **1** All computers on the Internet use a protocol called TCP/IP (Transmission Control Protocol/Internet Protocol). A *protocol* is a set of rules that lets computers agree how to communicate.

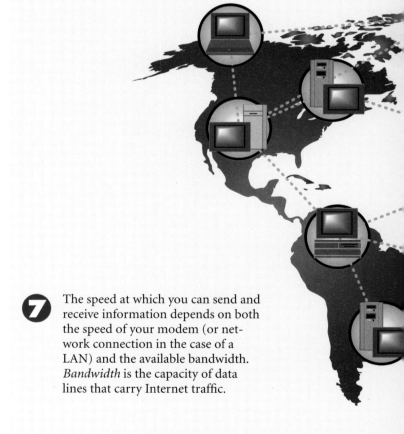

TIP SHEET

▸ **TCP/IP allows multiple computers to share the same connection. Even if you have a very fast modem, heavy traffic on the Internet may cause slow access times because the available bandwidth has to be divvied up among many users.**

▸ **In some areas of the country, you will soon be able to connect your home computer to the Internet using the same type of cable that's used for cable TV. This type of connection will be many times faster than either phone lines or ISDN.**

7 The speed at which you can send and receive information depends on both the speed of your modem (or network connection in the case of a LAN) and the available bandwidth. *Bandwidth* is the capacity of data lines that carry Internet traffic.

2 When you send a message across the Internet to another user, TCP divides the data into manageable units called *packets* and attaches to each packet the information necessary to reassemble the data and check for errors. IP then labels all the packets with a header containing the address of the destination, and sends them on their way. During the trip, specialized computers called *routers* work to direct the packets along the most efficient paths. (In fact, separate packets may travel on different paths toward the same destination.)

3 Once the packets reach their destination, the computer on the receiving end removes the IP header and uses the data that TCP attached to each packet to make sure none of the packets have been lost or damaged. The packets are then reassembled into the original message. If the computer discovers a damaged packet, it sends a message to the sending computer asking it to resend the packet.

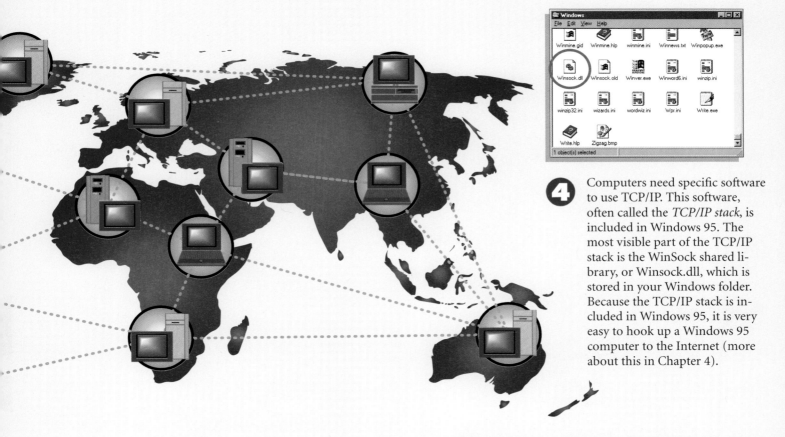

4 Computers need specific software to use TCP/IP. This software, often called the *TCP/IP stack*, is included in Windows 95. The most visible part of the TCP/IP stack is the WinSock shared library, or Winsock.dll, which is stored in your Windows folder. Because the TCP/IP stack is included in Windows 95, it is very easy to hook up a Windows 95 computer to the Internet (more about this in Chapter 4).

6 If you access the Internet from a computer at work, you are probably connecting through a company LAN that has a gateway to the Internet. A *gateway* is a special computer (often a router) on a LAN that is responsible for communicating between the LAN and the Internet at large. Where necessary, gateways translate between the protocol used internally on the LAN and TCP/IP, the protocol of the Internet.

5 The hardware used to connect computers to the Internet varies depending on the type of access you have. If you access the Internet from home, you most likely use a modem. (Modems let the computer send and receive information over the phone line.) Some people instead use a faster type of access called ISDN. (See Chapter 3 for more about the hardware required to access the Internet from home.)

How Does the World Wide Web Work?

O ne of the most distinctive aspects of the World Wide Web is that Web pages are usually linked; you can jump from one page to the next by clicking special text or images in the document. The ability to travel links is for the most part a good thing—you can easily explore related subjects, and you'll sometimes stumble onto real treasures you wouldn't have found otherwise. But you can run into trouble if you have even the slightest tendency toward being unfocused: Ten minutes into a concerted search for information about an upcoming ballot measure, you may discover that you're now studying a page of tips for making a dynamite cup of coffee. Here's a look at what's happening behind the links.

TIP SHEET

▶ **Increasingly, companies are using an additional protocol called SSL (Secure Sockets Layer) on their servers. This protocol encrypts data exchanged between the user and the Web site and keep it secure. You'll learn more about secure sites in Chapter 5.**

▶ **The idea of hypertext has actually been around for a long time. For example, online help systems in many application programs use hypertext to allow users to quickly jump from one part of the help system to another.**

Hypertext

LiveAudio - Hear music and voice directly from Web pages with embedded audio.

1 The "clickable" text indicating links on a Web page is called *hypertext*. It is usually underlined and displayed in a different color than the surrounding text; when you point to it with the mouse, your mouse pointer typically takes on the shape of a pointing hand. Clicking on a hypertext link refers your browser to the document or sound file or video clip to which the hypertext is linked.

5 Companies with Web sites usually maintain their own Web server, and there are also companies that maintain Web servers for other companies.

4 Remember, Web pages reside on Web servers. A Web server is normally a fast computer with a lot of disk space that is running special server software. Most people who maintain Web sites from home rent space for their Web pages on a Web server managed by an Internet service provider (ISP). This makes your pages available all the time without the expense of keeping your own computer online 24 hours a day. (You'll learn more about ISPs in Chapters 3 and 4.)

2 The Web uses a protocol called HTTP (Hypertext Transfer Protocol) to transfer documents containing hypertext. HTTP plays a role on the Web that's very similar to the role TCP/IP plays on the Internet as a whole—both protocols tell computers how to communicate with one another.

3 You create Web documents using a markup language called HTML (Hypertext Markup Language). HTML is really just a set of codes you use both to format the appearance of Web pages and to create links. (Chapters 18 through 20 teach you enough HTML to create simple Web pages.) To a browser, the HTML code for a Web page is like an instruction sheet telling it how to display the page. Here is a portion of the HTML code for a Web page, along with the actual page as viewed through a browser.

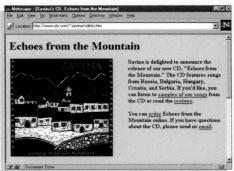

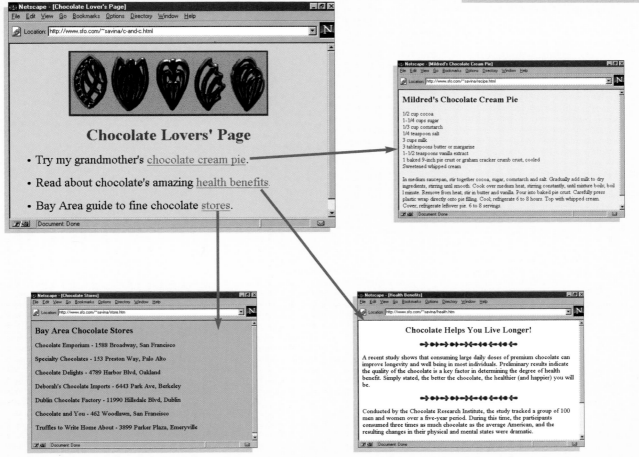

Understanding E-Mail Addresses

E-mail addresses function like postal addresses. Just as the address you write on an envelope tells the postal service where to send your letter, the e-mail address tells the Internet where to send your e-mail message. You'll learn the specifics of sending and receiving e-mail in Chapters 8 and 9, but learning a bit about e-mail addresses now will help you understand the structure of the Internet.

All e-mail addresses contain this symbol.

clinton@whitehouse.gov

▶ ❶ It's easy to recognize Internet e-mail addresses because they always contain an @ (pronounced "at") symbol. Here is President Clinton's e-mail address.

TIP SHEET

▶ E-mail addresses are not case sensitive and never contain any spaces.

▶ Each domain on the Internet has a computer that runs a nameserver program. *Nameservers* translate the name of each host computer from the word name you use in an e-mail address into a series of numbers (called the *IP address*) that the Internet uses to uniquely identify each host. Luckily we don't have to type these numbers directly!

User name

clinton@whitehouse.gov

2 The part of the address to the left of the @ symbol is the user name. This is the name the person uses to connect to his or her Internet account. Often user names are some combination of a person's first and last names.

Host and/or domain

clinton@whitehouse.gov

3 The part of the address to the right of the @ symbol is the mail destination. This part can vary quite a bit. Some addresses list both the host and the domain. The *host* is the computer that houses the Internet account, and the *domain* is the network to which the host computer is connected. In the address steele@itsa.ucsf.edu, the host is *itsa*, and the domain is *ucsf*. Other addresses include the domain but not the host—for example, in the address savina@sfo.com, *sfo* is the domain.

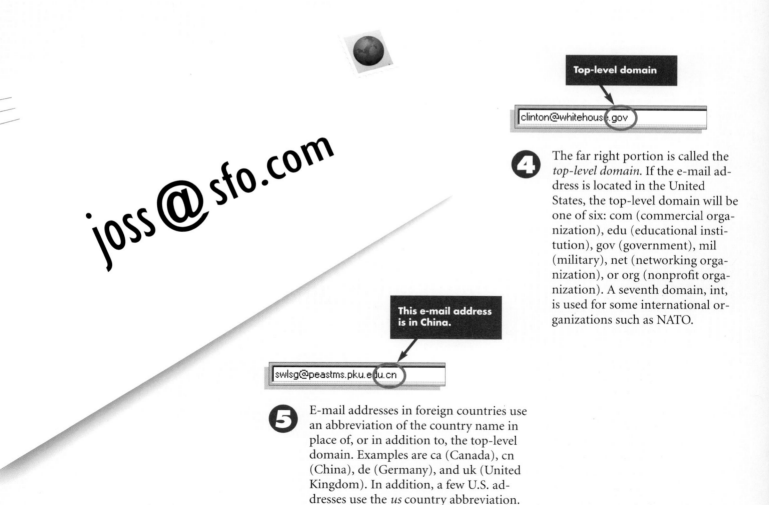

joss@sfo.com

Top-level domain

clinton@whitehouse.gov

4 The far right portion is called the *top-level domain*. If the e-mail address is located in the United States, the top-level domain will be one of six: com (commercial organization), edu (educational institution), gov (government), mil (military), net (networking organization), or org (nonprofit organization). A seventh domain, int, is used for some international organizations such as NATO.

This e-mail address is in China.

swlsg@peastms.pku.edu.cn

5 E-mail addresses in foreign countries use an abbreviation of the country name in place of, or in addition to, the top-level domain. Examples are ca (Canada), cn (China), de (Germany), and uk (United Kingdom). In addition, a few U.S. addresses use the *us* country abbreviation.

Understanding URLs

URLs identify locations on the Internet. Most typically you'll use URLs to jump to a specific site, but every individual item on the Internet—whether it's a Web page, a sound file, or a graphic image—also has its own URL. Most URLs point to Web sites, but you can also use URLs to access other Internet resources.

▶ **1** The first part of a URL indicates what protocol the browser should use to access the Internet site. Typical options for this part of the URL are http: (for Web sites), ftp: (for FTP sites), gopher: (for gopher sites), telnet: (for telnet sites), news: (for newsgroups), and file: (for files located on your own computer).

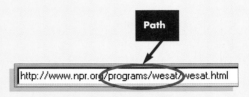

2 Following the protocol is the name of the Web server. In URLs for Web sites, this portion usually begins with www. This section technically ends with a forward slash, but you can usually omit the slash if you aren't specifying a particular document. (Once in a while, a browser may get confused if you omit the trailing slash. If this happens, type it in and try connecting again.)

http://www.library.org

http://www.hischool.edu

3 The third part of a URL is the path pointing to the specific part of the Web server that holds a particular document. The path begins and ends with a forward slash, and additional forward slashes are used to separate various parts of the path.

4 The fourth part of a URL is the specific name of the document. File names for Web pages end with the extension .htm or .html.

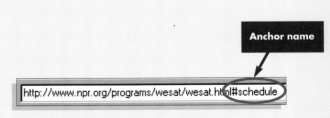

5 The fifth and final part of a URL is the *anchor name*, which is separated from the document name by a # symbol. You'll see anchor names in URLs that point to a specific section of a long Web page.

6 You only need to use the first two parts of a URL (described in steps 1 and 2) to get to a particular site. You enter the remaining parts only if you want to jump directly to a document at that site. In many cases, it's easier to jump to the "top level" of a Web site first, and then use links in the Web pages to get to specific documents. This strategy beats having to type URLs that are a mile long.

CHAPTER 3

How Do I Connect to the Internet?

Over the past few years, it has gotten progressively easier to connect to the Internet. With the arrival of Windows 95, the steps have become so simple that even average folk (those of us without degrees in computer science) can muddle our way through. This chapter and the next guide you through this process, and by the end of Chapter 4, you'll be up and running on the Internet.

There are two things I'd like to mention before we forge ahead: First, I assume you have a stand-alone computer running Windows 95. Second, if you can already get on the Internet from a computer at work that is on your company network and don't want to access the Internet on a home computer, you can skip this chapter and the next and go directly to Chapter 5, "Browsing the Web."

This chapter begins with a brief overview of the hardware you need for Internet access. It then outlines the two primary ways to connect your home computer to the Internet: through an online service such as America Online or CompuServe, or through an Internet service provider (ISP). As you'll see, my preference is to use an ISP, so that's the method you'll learn in detail in Chapter 4. Although this process is more involved than using an online service, it is much less expensive, and it gives you greater flexibility in choosing your browser and other Internet software.

What Hardware Do I Need for Internet Access?

The most common method of linking a home computer to the Internet is to use a modem. A modem allows your computer to send and receive information over the phone line by translating data between the analog signal that's used on the phone line and the digital signal that's used inside the computer. Most new computers come with built-in modems, but if you have an older computer you may need to buy one yourself. If you buy a modem, you can either install it yourself—it's not too difficult—or have someone at the computer store install it for you. You need to have a modem installed and working properly before continuing with Chapter 4.

TIP SHEET

▶ **If the phone line you're using for your modem has call waiting, you need to make sure call waiting won't interfere when you're connected to the Internet. To do this, double-click on the My Computer icon on your desktop, double-click on the Control Panel folder, and then double-click on the Modems icon. Click on the Dialing Properties button, and mark the check box This Location Has Call Waiting. Enter the code to disable call waiting in the text box (or select one from the drop-down list), and click on OK.**

▶ **ISDN is fairly expensive. The hardware alone can cost $300 to $400, and the base monthly rate from the phone company runs anywhere from $25 to $100, not including any per-minute charges. (This monthly fee is in addition to the monthly fee you pay your Internet service provider.) These costs are worthwhile if you are setting up Internet access for a small business, or if you plan on using your home computer as a Web server.**

▶ **❶** There are two types of modems: internal and external. An internal modem is a card that sits inside of your computer and connects to the phone line via a plug at the back of the computer case. Internal modems are usually a little less expensive than external ones and they are a bit more convenient because you don't have to turn them on, and they don't take up any space on your desk.

❽ In addition to a modem, you should have at least a 486 computer with 16MB of memory and 25MB of free hard-disk space. If you try to get by with anything less, you'll inevitably have some agonizingly long waits while accessing sites and downloading files.

❼ If you think you'll be spending a lot of time online, it's a great idea to get a second phone line just for your modem. Otherwise, the modem and the telephone will share the same line, and friends and coworkers may complain they get a busy signal whenever they call.

2 An external modem is a small box that sits next to your computer. You plug the phone line into the modem and use a cable to connect the modem to one of the serial ports on the back of your computer. Some people prefer external modems because they have a display panel with flashing lights that give you information about the status of your connection. Another advantage of external modems is that you can share them among several computers.

3 The most important consideration when buying a modem is speed. You should get at least a 28.8 Kbps modem if you want to access Web sites without pulling your hair out waiting for pages to appear. (Kbps stands for *kilobytes per second*, and it measures how fast data can be transmitted across the line.) A 28.8 Kbps or V.34 modem, commonly referred to as a "twenty-eight eight," costs around $200.

4 A more costly option that allows faster access speeds than a 28.8 modem is a service called ISDN (Integrated Services Digital Network). ISDN allows the phone line to carry information in digital rather than analog format and can reach transfer speeds of up to 128 Kbps. This service is probably available from your phone company, although you may have to hunt for someone who can help you set it up. Furthermore, ISDN can be somewhat difficult to configure because the pricing and service options are not yet standardized.

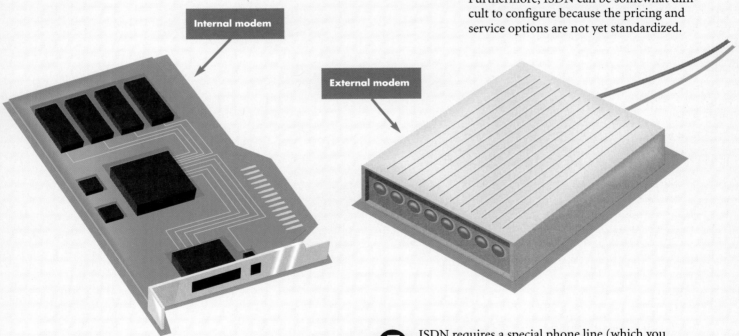

Internal modem

External modem

6 Two other options for connecting to the Internet that are far faster than ISDN are ADSL (Asymmetric Digital Subscriber Line) and cable modems. While neither of these technologies is widely available yet, some people predict that one of them will eventually become the standard, leaving ISDN by the wayside.

5 ISDN requires a special phone line (which you get from your phone company) and either an internal card, called a *terminal adapter*, or an external ISDN modem, both of which you can buy from a computer hardware store. (An ISDN modem isn't a "modem" per se because it doesn't translate data between analog and digital formats. Nonetheless, it *looks* like a modem, hence the technically incorrect name.)

Connecting through an Online Service

Online services such as America Online (AOL), CompuServe, the Microsoft Network (MSN), and Prodigy are self-contained communities that provide a wealth of resources to their members—news, software, online banking, discussion groups, e-mail, and so on. Now that the Internet is so popular, such services have had to scramble to add Internet access or risk losing customers. All of them now have gateways to the Internet that include access to the World Wide Web, and they all provide their own browser software.

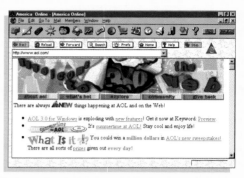

1 America Online's software (version 2.5 or later) includes AOL's own Web browser. After you sign on to AOL, you use the Internet Connection button to access Internet and Web resources.

TIP SHEET

▶ Some online services also function as Internet service providers, meaning that they offer direct Internet accounts (see the next page) that *don't* include access to their online service. AOL, for example, offers Internet access through a company called GNN (Global Network Navigator). See the next page for more about connecting through an Internet service provider.

▶ America Online lets you use other browsers than its own, although it can be tricky to set this up. CompuServe is planning to move its entire service to the Web. Both of these services are in a state of transition as they try to find their niche on the Web.

7 Finally, these online services are so large that it can be quite difficult to find a real human being to help you when you need technical support.

6 Another problem is that you will be charged for the time you spend on the Internet, just as you are for the time you spend using the online service itself. Given how easy it is to putter on the Internet, this time can really add up, and you may end up with a nasty surprise when your bill arrives at the end of the month.

2 If you are a CompuServe member, you can use the Windows version of the CompuServe Information Manager, WinCIM (version 2.0.1 or later), to access the Internet. WinCIM comes with CompuServe's version of the Mosaic Web browser. First you have to use CompuServe's dialer program to establish your Internet connection; then you can launch the Mosaic browser.

3 If you are a member of the Microsoft Network, you can go to the Internet Center after you've signed in. From there, you use the Internet Explorer (Microsoft's browser) to browse the Web.

4 Prodigy for Windows software (as of version 1.1) includes Prodigy's own Web browser. To use it, specify Web Browser as your connection when you sign onto Prodigy.

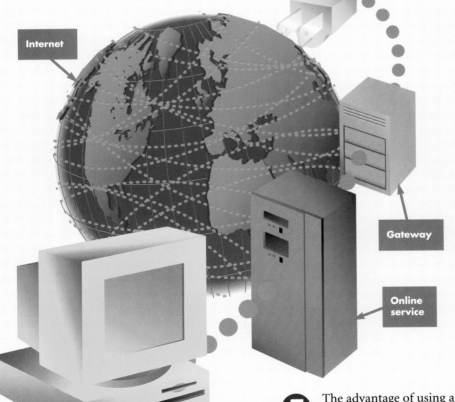

5 The advantage of using an online service for Internet access is that it takes little or no setup. Unfortunately, there are also major drawbacks to going this route. One problem is that the browsers furnished by the services (with the exception of MSN, which by default uses Microsoft's browser, Internet Explorer) don't do a particularly good job of displaying Web pages. Pages that look wonderful when viewed through Netscape or Internet Explorer may look off kilter or lack important formatting when viewed through the online service's browser.

Connecting through an Internet Service Provider

Internet service providers (also called *Internet access providers*) offer Internet access to their customers for a monthly fee. ISPs range in size from small, local companies with fewer than 2,000 users to nationwide operations with over 30,000 users. The ISP's computers are connected to the Internet 24 hours a day. When you establish an account with an ISP, you receive a local access number that you use to dial into their computer system. (If you live far from an urban center, you may have to use a long distance access number.) When your computer is connected to the ISP, you have access to the Internet and the World Wide Web.

▶ ❶ Most ISPs provide more than one type of dial-up connection to the Internet. The type of connection you want is called PPP (Point-to-Point Protocol); this is also referred to as a *direct* Internet connection. With PPP, TCP/IP travels down the phone line to your computer, enabling your computer to communicate with other computers on the Internet. A PPP connection also lets you browse graphical documents on the Web. ISPs normally assume new users want PPP, but you should still confirm that's what you're getting.

TIP SHEET

▶ Many older Internet accounts are *shell* accounts. Unlike PPP accounts, these accounts don't establish a direct connection between your computer and the Internet. Consequently, they can't run TCP/IP, and they don't let you view graphical documents on the Web. With a shell account, your computer merely functions as a terminal connected to the host computer (a UNIX machine), which is itself directly connected to the Internet. Many students and faculty at universities still use this type of account.

▶ A few ISPs use a protocol similar to PPP called SLIP (Serial Line Internet Protocol). While SLIP also brings TCP/IP through the phone line and gives you a direct Internet connection, it's an older, less reliable protocol than PPP.

▶ The next chapter discusses ISPs in more depth. You'll get some pointers on how to choose an ISP as well as detailed instructions for setting up your Internet connection.

2 Many ISPs offer 24-hour unlimited access to the Internet for a fixed monthly fee, which usually ranges from $15 to $35. With this type of access, you can browse to your heart's content without watching the clock. (This may or may not please your boss, family, and friends.)

3 Some ISPs throw in free Web space on their server with their standard PPP accounts. This is a great bonus if you intend to set up your own Web site.

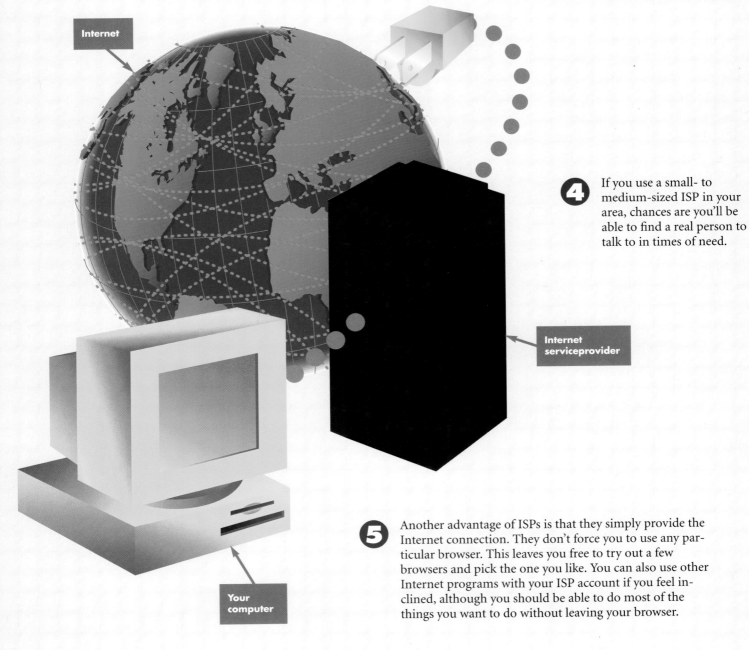

Internet

Internet serviceprovider

Your computer

4 If you use a small- to medium-sized ISP in your area, chances are you'll be able to find a real person to talk to in times of need.

5 Another advantage of ISPs is that they simply provide the Internet connection. They don't force you to use any particular browser. This leaves you free to try out a few browsers and pick the one you like. You can also use other Internet programs with your ISP account if you feel inclined, although you should be able to do most of the things you want to do without leaving your browser.

CHAPTER 4

Setting Up an Account with an ISP

From choosing an Internet Service Provider to creating a connection to the ISP and setting up your browser, this chapter tells you everything you need to know to connect to the Internet from home.

First, you get some suggestions for finding an ISP you like, and then you learn what specific pieces of information you need to get from your ISP before setting up your connection.

Next, you learn how to create a dial-up connection to your ISP. One approach is to buy the Windows 95 add-on called Plus!, which contains an *Internet Setup wizard*. This wizard prompts you for information about your ISP, which it then plugs into the relevant Windows 95 dialog boxes. But this method shields you from the Windows 95 dialog boxes containing Internet-related information. This makes things difficult if you later need to check or change a setting, because you'll have no idea where to find it. Fortunately, Windows 95 has everything you need to connect to the Internet, so this chapter tells you how to configure a connection without using Plus!

Finally, you learn how to install and configure Netscape Navigator.

You should at least skim this chapter before you start talking to ISPs. That way, the information they give you will make more sense. Also note that every ISP has different hardware, so some might need you to configure things a little differently than the standard setup described in this chapter.

Finding an Internet Service Provider

One of the best ways to find a good ISP is to ask for recommendations from Internet-savvy friends in your area. The free computer magazines available in many cities are another source of information about ISPs. You can also try looking in the Yellow Pages under Computers-Online Services or Computers-Internet. If you have access to the Web through a friend or at work, another option is to check out the many online directories of ISPs. One particularly good list, appropriately called The List, is at http://thelist.com. This page gives you some pointers for finding an ISP that suits your needs.

TIP SHEET

▶ You may want to ask about the bandwidth capacity of an ISP's connection to the Internet. However, there is no hard-and-fast rule about this, because the feasibility of providing high-capacity bandwidth varies by region. In urban areas, even small ISPs are likely to use high-capacity lines. In contrast, ISPs of the same size in rural areas would be hard pressed to provide comparable service, because high-capacity lines may not be available or may be prohibitively expensive.

▶ You may want to consider whether the domain name of an ISP is easy to remember, because it will be used in your e-mail address and URL (unless you pay extra to get your own domain name). Your aunt in Florida is more likely to remember a domain name like sfo.com than ogopikom.ssoj.com.

▶ If you are considering using a large ISP, ask about your chances of getting your first choice for a user name. The larger the ISP, the more likely it is that someone in the ISP's domain is already using the name you want, especially if you have a name like Susan Smith. Along these lines, you should also avoid ISPs that want to assign you a name.

▶ **1** The large ISPs can afford to maintain highly *fault tolerant* systems, meaning that they have redundant equipment to ensure that the system stays up and running and your data is protected no matter what. This is an important consideration if you intend to maintain an extensive Web site. It probably isn't as critical if you don't plan to have a Web site at all, or if your site will be small.

2 One potential problem with using a large ISP is that you aren't likely to get the personal technical support that's frequently available from small, local providers. As an example of good service, San Francisco Online, a local ISP with fewer than 1,000 users (http://www.sfo.com), provides tech support seven days a week. During the work week, they answer calls from the early morning hours until late at night to make it easier for people who are at work during the day to get help. If possible, you should look for an ISP that provides similar service.

3 Consider asking how long the ISP has been in business and how much they've grown. If they've been in business for several years but haven't grown at all, chances are they have a high attrition rate, which in all likelihood means their service is less than spectacular. If the ISP is brand new, they are probably still working out the kinks in their system, so you might be in for a bumpy ride.

4 Check whether the ISP can support many different platforms (Mac, Windows 3.1, Windows 95, Windows NT, several flavors of UNIX, and so on). If they can, it's a good indication that they have a thorough knowledge of computers and networks.

5 If you want to create your own Web site, ask whether the ISP provides any free Web space with their accounts, and if so, how many megabytes. (Just to give you a feeling for size requirements, 10MB is plenty for a small site that doesn't have a large number of graphics or other multimedia files.)

7 It's a good idea to ask the ISP how often their users get a busy signal and how long users have to wait after a busy signal before they can get through. Better yet, you can ask the ISP if they'll let you try out the service for a few days at no charge (some will). That way, you can see for yourself how easy it is to connect.

6 Find out what the monthly fee is. You should look for an ISP that charges a flat rate for unlimited 24-hour access. Prices usually range from $15 to $40 per month.

Gathering Information from Your Internet Service Provider

O nce you've chosen an ISP, the next step is to ask the ISP for some pieces of information that you need to set up your connection to the ISP. (A reasonably well-organized ISP should have this information all ready to give you.) Write down the information and have it next to your computer as you follow the remaining steps in this chapter.

▶ **1** Find out the local access number. This is the phone number your modem dials to connect to your ISP.

8 Ask for the name of the news server, also called the *NNTP* (Network News Transfer Protocol) *server*. This is the server your ISP uses to handle Usenet newsgroups.

7 Ask for the names of the outgoing mail server, also called the *SMTP* (Simple Mail Transfer Protocol) *server* and the incoming mail server, also called the *POP* (Post Office Protocol) *server*. The name may be the same for both—an example is mail@sfo.com. These are the names of the servers your ISP uses to handle e-mail.

TIP SHEET

▶ **If your ISP gives you some information not specifically mentioned here, write it down and find out where you enter it. (It will go in some dialog box in Windows 95 or your browser.) There is some variation in how ISPs set up their systems, so it's possible you'll have to jot down another item or two.**

2 Choose a user name and a password. Your ISP will ask you for these when you sign up. Choose a password that includes numbers and/or punctuation to make it harder to guess. There's also a possibility that the ISP will assign you a password. Be sure to keep your password secret.

3 Find out what your e-mail address will be.

4 If you are going to set up a Web site, make sure to ask what the URL for your site will be. A very common URL for sites on ISP machines is http://*your_isp_machine*/~*username*. A good example of this type of URL is the URL for my choir's Web site, http://www.sfo.com/~savina

5 Ask for the ISP's IP addresses of the primary and secondary DNS servers. Each address will be a series of digits separated by periods (for example, 207.182.15.50).

6 Confirm that the ISP will dynamically assign the IP address for your computer. If, by chance, the ISP gives you a static IP address, write it down. Typically, the ISP dynamically assigns a different IP address to your computer each time you connect. (When you make a PPP connection to your ISP, your computer temporarily becomes a part of the Internet, so it has to have an IP address to identify itself to other Internet computers.)

Information from Internet Service Provider

☑ Local access number

☑ User name and password

☑ Your e-mail address

☑ Your URL (if you plan to create a Web site)

☑ Primary and secondary DNS numbers

☑ Method of assigning IP address

☑ Names of mail servers

Creating a Connection to Your Internet Service Provider

Once you've gathered the information from your ISP, you need to create a connection to that ISP in Windows 95. To do so, you'll use a Windows 95 feature called Dial-Up Networking. To check if it's installed, click on the Start button, point to Settings, and click on Control Panel. Double-click on Add/Remove Programs, click on the Windows Setup tab, select the Communications option and click on the Details button. If the Dial-Up Networking check box is marked, it's already installed. If it isn't, mark the box and click on OK. Windows will prompt you for your setup disks or CD so that it can install the missing files.

▶ **1** Click on the Start button, point to Programs, point to Accessories, and click on Dial-Up Networking. In the Dial-Up Networking window, double-click on the Make New Connection icon to start the Make New Connection wizard.

8 Finally, to confirm that Windows 95 will use the new connection automatically, double-click on the My Computer icon on the Windows 95 desktop, double-click on Control Panel, and then double-click on the Internet icon. Make sure that the Use AutoDial check box is marked and that your new connection is selected under Settings. Then click on OK.

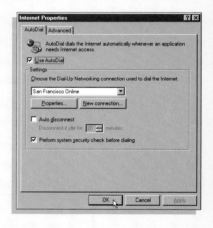

TIP SHEET

► It's a good idea to set up your Internet connection during your ISP's business hours, so that you can call your ISP if you're missing any key pieces of information.

► You can create a shortcut icon for your Internet connection on the Windows desktop. Then you simply double-click on the icon whenever you want to connect to your ISP. To create the shortcut, double-click on the My Computer icon, and then double-click on the Dial-Up Networking icon. *Right*-drag the icon for your Internet connection onto the desktop and choose Create Shortcut(s) Here from the context menu.

► If you don't create a shortcut for your Internet connection, you can still dial your ISP by double-clicking on the icon for your connection in the Dial-Up Networking window (shown in step 4).

7 Leave the Server Assigned IP Address option button marked if your ISP dynamically assigns your IP address. Assuming your ISP gave you permanent DNS addresses, mark the Specify Name Server Addresses option button and fill in the Primary DNS and Secondary DNS numbers. Leave the check boxes labeled Use IP Header Compression and Use Default Gateway on Remote Network marked, and click on OK twice to close both this dialog box and the previous one.

2 Type a name in the text box labeled Type a Name for the Computer You Are Dialing. You'll probably want to use the name of the ISP here. Make sure the correct modem type is selected, and click on the Next button.

3 Enter the local access number in the Area Code and Telephone Number text boxes. Then click on the Next button. In the final wizard dialog box, click on the Finish button to close the wizard and create the new connection.

My Internet Connection

4 Now that you've created the connection, you need to give it more information about your ISP. The Dial-Up Networking window will include a new icon for the connection you just created. Right-click on the icon to display a context menu, and choose Properties.

6 At the top of the Server Types dialog box, make sure the default setting of PPP: Windows 95, Windows NT 3.5, Internet is selected. Mark the Enable Software Compression check box, and clear the other two check boxes under Advanced Options. Under Allowed Network Protocols, mark the TCP/IP check box and clear the other two. Next, click on the TCP/IP Settings button.

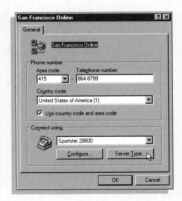

5 The dialog box that appears will contain the phone number and modem information you already entered. Click on the Server Type button.

Installing and Configuring Netscape

The final step in establishing an Internet connection is to install and configure your browser. This page assumes you bought Netscape Navigator and are installing it from floppy disks. (See the tip on this page for information on downloading Netscape Navigator from Netscape's Web site.)

▶ **If you bought Netscape Navigator at a store, you probably have the Personal Edition. This version comes with an account setup wizard, which helps new users create an Internet connection and configure Netscape. If you are following along in this book, you don't need to use this wizard (although you still need to register the software). Netscape Navigator Gold, a more expensive version of Netscape available at Netscape's Web site, includes an editor for creating Web pages.**

▶ **If you already have access to the Web, you can download the current version of Netscape Navigator from Netscape's Web site at http://home.netscape.com. (See Chapter 6 for help.) If you are installing a downloaded copy of Netscape, you may be asked to connect to Netscape's Web site to complete the setup process and register the software. After following those instructions, continue with step 5 on this page.**

▶ **Note that simply closing the Netscape program window does not disconnect you from your ISP. To actually break the phone connection, you need to click the Disconnect button in the Connected message box, as shown in step 8. (If you want your ISP connection to automatically disconnect after a specified length of time with no activity, right-click on the icon for your connection in the Dial-Up Networking folder, click on Properties, click on Configure, click on the Connection Tab, mark the check box Disconnect a Call If Idle for More Than 30 Mins, change the number of minutes if desired, and then click on OK twice.)**

▶ ❶ Insert Disk 1 of the Netscape Navigator setup disks in your floppy drive, click on the Start button, click on Run, type **a:\setup**, and press Enter. Then follow the onscreen prompts to complete the installation process.

❽ That's it! When you're ready to disconnect from your ISP, click on the button for your ISP connection on the Windows taskbar, click on the Disconnect button, and then close the Netscape program window.

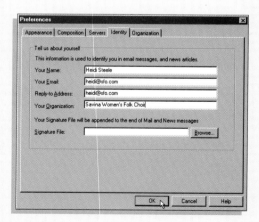

❼ Click on the Identity tab in the Preferences dialog box, and fill in the Your Name, Your Email, Reply-to Address, and Your Organization text boxes. (The Reply-to Address is normally the same as your e-mail address.)

2 As part of the installation, Netscape creates a shortcut for Netscape Navigator on the Windows desktop. Double-click on the short-cut to launch the browser.

3 Because you enabled AutoDial (see step 8 on the previous page), the Connect To dialog box appears as soon as Netscape starts. Type your user name and password, and then click on the Connect button. (Windows will remember your user name in the future, so you won't have to type it again.)

4 A message box will state that your com-puter is connecting to your ISP. Once the connection is established and your user name and password have been verified, Windows briefly displays (and then mini-mizes) the Connected message box to in-dicate that you are currently online.

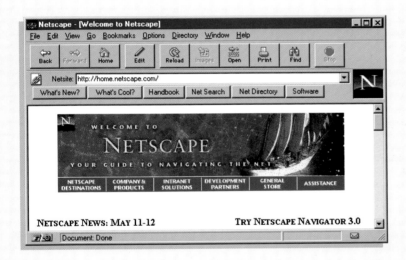

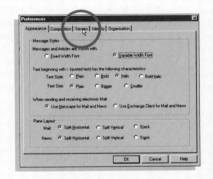

5 By default, Netscape connects you to its own Web site (shown in the middle of this page). You'll learn how to use Netscape to browse other sites in the next chapter. Before you start playing on the Web, however, you need to give Netscape some information about your ISP. To do this, choose the Mail and News Preferences com-mand in the Options menu to dis-play the Preferences dialog box, and then click on the Servers tab.

6 Enter the incoming and outgoing mail server names and the POP user name. (Unless your ISP told you otherwise, your POP user name is the same as your regular user name.) Then enter the name for the news server.

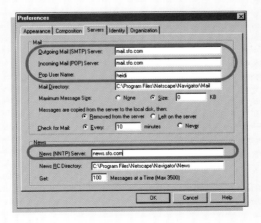

CHAPTER 5

Browsing the Web

One day, browsing the Web will be as commonplace as browsing the Yellow Pages, and navigating cyberspace will be as easy as walking to the corner store. But we're not there yet, so a few pointers on how to get around will help your browsing go more smoothly. Another pragmatic reason for becoming an expert at efficient browsing is that even with a fast modem, accessing the Web is still just plain slow. As we wait for data-transfer technology to catch up to the Web, learning the quickest way to get from point A to point B will help keep thumb-twiddling to a minimum.

This chapter begins with a lesson on the basics of displaying new Web pages. Then you get a grab bag of useful techniques for moving back and forth among Web pages you've already visited.

Next, you learn how to *bookmark* Web pages. This topic is a must-read, since bookmarks tell Netscape to remember the URLs for particular sites so you can get back to them easily. You also learn how to organize your bookmarks according to topic. If you get good at bookmarks, you can considerably reduce the number of Post-Its clinging to your monitor, and increase your efficiency to boot.

Sooner or later, you'll visit a page that's divided into multiple sections, or *frames*. This chapter explains what frames are and what to expect when you maneuver in them. It also introduces Java-enhanced pages—pages that contain mini programs (called *applets*) created using a language called Java.

Finally, you learn about all the options for saving and printing Web pages.

How to Display Web Pages

There are two basic ways to tell Netscape what page you want to retrieve. You can enter the URL for the page or click on a hypertext link (or a specific part of an image) that leads to the page. Also, if you visit one page frequently, you can instruct Netscape to display that page automatically on startup. The steps shown here assume you've already started Netscape. (If you haven't, double-click on the Netscape shortcut icon on the Windows desktop to start the program and connect to your ISP.)

▶ **1** If you know the URL for a page, you can enter it directly in the Location text box near the top of the Netscape window. To do this, first click anywhere in the text box to select the current URL. (If you don't see the Location text box, choose Options, Show Location.)

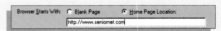

7 To the right of Browser Starts With, make sure the Home Page Location option button is selected, enter the desired URL in the text box, and click on OK. Now the specified page will be displayed whenever you start Netscape or click on the Home button.

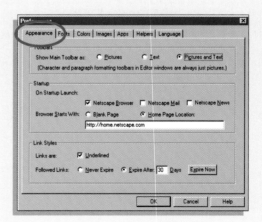

6 By default, the Netscape browser displays Netscape's own Web site when you first launch the program or when you click on the Home button in the toolbar. (If you don't see the toolbar, choose Options, Show Toolbar.) To change this default Web site, choose Options, General Preferences, and, if necessary, click on the Appearances tab at the top of the Preferences dialog box.

Go to: http://gagme.wwa.com/~boba/kidsi.html

2 Type the URL for the desired page. As soon as you begin typing, your text replaces the previous URL and the label for the Location text box changes to *Go to*. Press Enter to have Netscape retrieve the page. (If you click a second time before typing, you can place an insertion point in the existing URL and edit it rather than replacing it.)

Connect: Host miso.wwa.com contacted. Waiting for reply...

3 As Netscape is fetching a page, it displays messages about the status of the transfer in the status bar at the bottom of the Netscape window.

Home button   **Location text box**   **Open button**   **Find button**

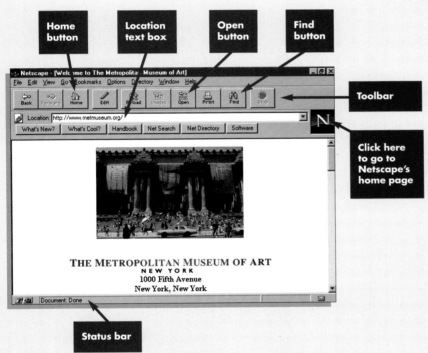

Toolbar

Click here to go to Netscape's home page

Status bar

4 Once the page is completely transferred, the status bar displays the message "Document: Done." This process can take anywhere from a couple of seconds to several minutes or more, depending on the speed of your modem, other network traffic, the location of the server holding the page, and the complexity of the page, among other things.

April
Passover Community Seder
Jewish Family Education Program
Journey to Jerusalem
Israel Independance Day Celebration
Koret Gallery Israel Exhibit
http://www.paloaltojcc.org/html/journey.html

5 The other way to display Web pages is to click on links. When you point to a link, the mouse pointer becomes a hand (in most browsers), and the URL of the page that will be retrieved appears in the status bar. Note that some links are embedded in graphic images. An image that contains links is known as an *image map*.

How to Navigate among Web Pages

O n the previous page, you learned how to travel to new areas of the Web. Here and on the next page, you learn techniques for quickly getting back to places you've already been, without having to remember or retype URLs. These methods are invaluable when you've accidentally followed links down the wrong road and want to retrace your steps.

▶ ❶ To move back to the previous page, click on the Back button on the toolbar (or press Alt+←). If you are viewing a previous page, you can return to the most recent page by clicking the Forward button (or by pressing Alt+→).

❽ Release the mouse button to create the shortcut icon. In the future, you can double-click on the shortcut to both start Netscape and jump to the page.

TIP SHEET

▶ If you select a URL in the Location text box and then double-click on the Chain Link button, Netscape copies the URL to the Windows clipboard. You can then paste the URL into any other application program, or even into an e-mail message (more about that in Chapter 9).

▶ You can also create a shortcut to a Web page by right-clicking on a page to display a context menu, and then choosing Internet Shortcut. In the Create Internet Shortcut dialog box that appears, edit the description or the URL if you choose, and click on OK.

Drag Chain Link button to create shortcut

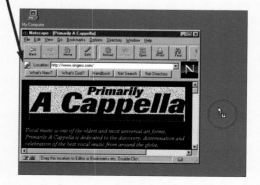

❼ Drag from the Chain Link button onto the desktop. Your mouse pointer changes into a small square containing a curved arrow.

2 Netscape keeps track of the last ten URLs you typed in the Location text box. If you want to return to one of these locations, click on the drop-down arrow at the right of the text box to display the list of URLs, and click on the one you want.

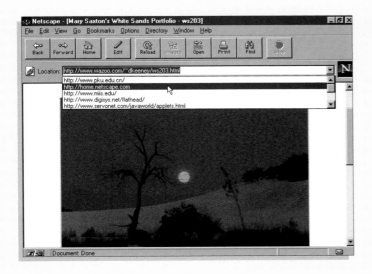

3 The bottom of the Go menu lists the pages you've visited in the current Netscape session. This list includes locations you reached by typing URLs in the Location text box, as well as those you visited by clicking links. To return to a page, just click on it.

4 If you entered a URL or clicked on a link and it's taking an intolerable amount of time to retrieve the page, you can stop the transfer by clicking on the Stop button on the toolbar.

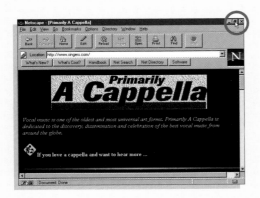

5 The Reload button is useful when a page didn't load properly or completely or if you want to retrieve a fresh copy from the server.

6 In Netscape 2.0 Gold and all the more recent versions of Netscape, a Chain Link button appears to the left of the Location text box. You can use this button to create a shortcut icon for a particular Web page on the Windows desktop. First display the page in question, and then, if necessary, click on the Restore button in the upper-right corner of the Netscape window so that some of the desktop is visible.

How to Use Bookmarks

Browsing the Web is an extremely nonlinear process. You may randomly follow a dozen or so links before reaching a page that tickles your fancy. As soon as you arrive at a page you think you'll want to visit again, bookmark it. Then you don't have to worry about writing down its URL or memorizing the trail of links that got you there.

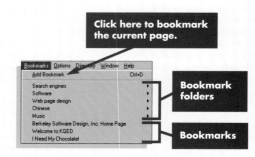

Click here to bookmark the current page.

Bookmark folders

Bookmarks

1 When you land on a page you'd like to bookmark, issue the Bookmarks, Add Bookmark command (or press Ctrl+D). This adds the bookmark to the bottom of the Bookmarks menu. To use the bookmark later, simply display the Bookmarks menu and click on the bookmark.

TIP SHEET

▶ **Typically, you'll add bookmarks to the Bookmarks menu as you are browsing, and then periodically go into the Bookmarks window to drag the new bookmarks into appropriate folders.**

▶ **You can add a new bookmark and place it in its correct folder in one step. To do this, display the Bookmarks window, and resize both it and the Netscape window so that the two windows are displayed side by side. When you want to bookmark a page, drag the Chain Link button (to the left of the Location text box) over to the desired folder in the Bookmarks window.**

▶ **To delete a bookmark, click on the bookmark in the Bookmarks window and press the Delete key.**

▶ **If you choose the File, What's New? command in the Bookmarks window, Netscape checks all the bookmarked pages (or the selected ones) to see if the content has changed since you last visited the page. It then indicates which pages have changed by displaying little yellow lines around the bookmark icons.**

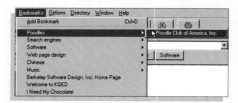

8 Once you've reorganized your bookmarks, drop down the Bookmarks menu again. You will see the new folders you created, and pointing to each one will display the submenu listing the individual bookmarks.

7 To move a bookmark into a new folder, drag the bookmark from its current location to the folder and release the mouse when the folder name is highlighted. Continue creating folders and moving bookmarks into them until you've brought some order to the chaos. When you're done, click on the Close button (the X) in the upper-right corner of the Bookmarks window to return to the Netscape window.

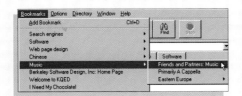

2 As you can imagine, the list of bookmarks in the Bookmarks menu can quickly become too long to be of much use. To organize your bookmarks in some logical way and shorten the list in the Bookmarks menu at the same time, you can create bookmark folders (or even folders within folders). Netscape places folder names near the top of the Bookmarks menu with black triangles to their right. When you point to a folder name, a sub-menu appears with the bookmarks in that folder.

3 To create folders, start by choosing Bookmarks from the Window menu (or pressing Ctrl+B). This displays the Bookmarks window.

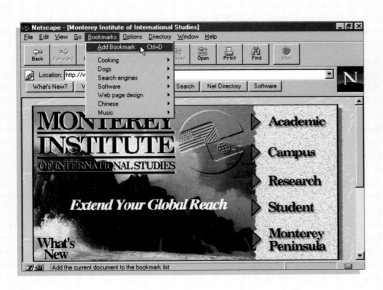

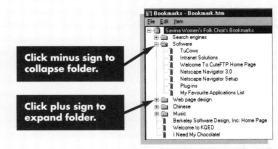

Click minus sign to collapse folder.

Click plus sign to expand folder.

4 Notice that folders are shown with small plus or minus signs. Clicking on a plus sign displays all the bookmarks in a folder; clicking on a minus sign hides the bookmarks in a folder.

6 In the Bookmark Properties dialog box, type a name for the folder and optionally enter a description. Then click on OK.

5 To create a new folder, click on the top line in the Bookmarks window (the name of the bookmarks file directly underneath the menu bar) and choose Item, Insert Folder from within the Bookmarks window.

How to View Sites with Frames

As you're wandering around the Web, you're sure to come across many sites that use frames. Frames are independent scrollable panes within a Web page. They are useful for two reasons: First, they let the Web designer place information in a pane that stays visible regardless of where the user has scrolled in the page. Second, the contents of multiple frames can be interlinked, so that clicking on a link in one frame retrieves the linked information into a separate frame.

 The Web site shown here, for Montana's Flathead valley (http://www.fcva.org/flathead), is divided into three separate frames.

2 The frame at the top is a *ledge*—a frame that always stays visible and stationary as you navigate in the frames underneath. Companies frequently use ledges to display their name and logo.

3 Like many sites that employ frames, this one uses a frame on the left to list the main categories of information at the site. When you click on a category (Communities, in this example), related information is displayed in the frame to the right.

4 You can further manipulate the contents of the right-hand frame by clicking on the subcategories in the area just above it (Bigfork, Columbia Falls, and so on).

5 Netscape Navigator 2.0 was the first browser to recognize frames, and Internet Explorer followed suit. Some other less-popular browsers still don't recognize frames.

How to View Java-Enhanced Sites

If you've visited sites that play sounds, have animated figures trotting across the screen, or display scrolling text, you've already seen Java at work. Developed by Sun Microsystems, Java is a programming language that developers use to create *applets*, small programs that are embedded in Web pages and that run when a user accesses the page or clicks on a certain area. You don't have to *do* anything to view sites that contain Java, except be patient, since pages with Java tend to load more slowly.

▶ ❶ One small Java applet that many Web pages now use creates "ticker-tape" text that runs across the screen. In this example, the text in the blimp graphic is continuously scrolling.

❼ At the moment, Netscape and Internet Explorer are the only popular browsers that understand Java. Another less well-known browser specifically designed to view Java applets is HotJava from Sun Microsystems (http://javasoft.com).

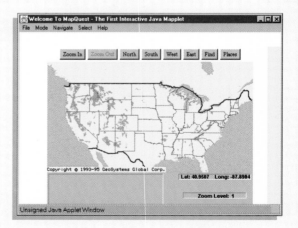

❻ You can zoom in and out to change your view of the map, and can request information concerning points of interest, lodging, and restaurants in any part of the country.

2 Java development is still in the experimental stages. As a result, you'll probably see a lot of cute (but not particularly practical) Java-based animations. In this example, the earth bounces randomly around the shaded background. Along the same lines, the little guy standing in front of the letter *J* in the center of this page, whose name is Duke, scampers around many Java programmers' Web pages. Duke is the Java mascot, and he's been a member of the development team at Sun since the beginning.

3 There are also a growing number of serious Java applications on the Web. One, called WallStreetWeb (http://www.bulletproof.com/Wall StreetWeb), was developed by Bulletproof Corporation to help people track stocks.

5 Another applet, called Java Interactive Atlas, was developed by Geosystems and is available at http://www.mapquest.com.

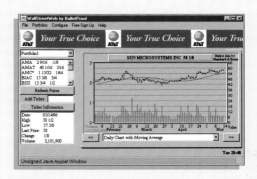

4 WallStreetWeb displays updated stock information in real time, and lets you make a wide variety of selections to customize the data included in the display.

Saving and Printing Web Pages

In your travels around the Web, you will occasionally come across information that you'd like to save to disk. You might want to save pages you refer to frequently, because opening a file from disk is usually much faster than connecting to a Web site. Also, the Web includes many archives of photographs and graphic images. To use these images in your own documents, you need to first save them to disk. Netscape lets you save entire Web pages in a couple of different formats. You can also save the graphic images from Web pages, or save just a portion of a Web page by doing a little cutting and pasting. Alternatively, you can print Web pages from your browser without saving them to disk.

TIP SHEET

▶ **If you save an HTML file from the Web and then open it in a word processing program, the document won't display as it does in a browser; instead, you will see all the actual HTML codes.**

▶ **If you right-click on a link, Netscape displays a context menu containing the Save Link As command. Choosing this command saves the linked page without retrieving it to the screen. (You can also do this by holding down the Shift key as you click on the link.)**

▶ **If you want to save the contents of a frame, click inside the frame once to make it active, and then choose File, Save Frame As. You can print the contents of an individual frame by clicking on it and choosing Print, Print Frame. (When a page containing frames is displayed, the Save As and Print commands become Save Frame As and Print Frame.)**

  When you want to save an entire Web page, display the page, and then choose File, Save As to bring up the Save As dialog box.

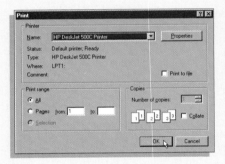

 To print a Web page, display the page in Netscape, click on the Print toolbar button (or choose File, Print) to bring up the Print dialog box, and click on OK.

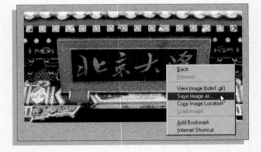

If a Web page contains a graphic image you'd like to save, right-click anywhere on the image to display a context menu, and choose Save Image As to bring up the standard Save As dialog box. You won't need to choose a format for graphic files because Netscape automatically retains the original format—either GIF or JPG. (You'll learn about formats for graphic images in Chapter 20.)

2 If you want to preserve the page formatting, leave HTML Files selected in the Save As Type drop-down list to have Netscape save the Web page with all its HTML codes. You can later use any browser to view the file (in Netscape, choose File, Open File), which will appear as it did when Netscape retrieved it from the Web site. Note, however, that Netscape does not automatically save graphic images contained in Web pages. See step 7 to learn how to save graphics.

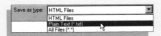

3 To save the Web page as plain text without any of its original formatting, choose the Plain Text option in the Save As Type list box.

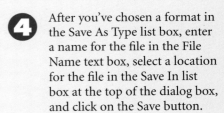

4 After you've chosen a format in the Save As Type list box, enter a name for the file in the File Name text box, select a location for the file in the Save In list box at the top of the dialog box, and click on the Save button.

5 The Saving Location message box appears briefly as Netscape saves the Web page.

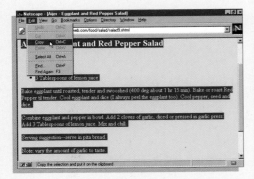

6 If you want to save only a portion of the text in a Web page, highlight it first by dragging over it with the mouse. Choose Edit, Copy to copy the selected text to the Windows clipboard, start your word processing program, and use its Edit, Paste command to paste the text into any document. You can then save and/or print the text.

CHAPTER 6

Downloading and Installing Software

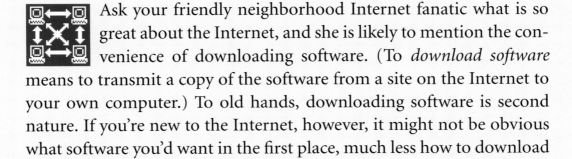Ask your friendly neighborhood Internet fanatic what is so great about the Internet, and she is likely to mention the convenience of downloading software. (To *download software* means to transmit a copy of the software from a site on the Internet to your own computer.) To old hands, downloading software is second nature. If you're new to the Internet, however, it might not be obvious what software you'd want in the first place, much less how to download and install it. This chapter will answer these questions—when you're through reading it, you'll be able to download with the best of them.

First, you learn what types of software most people download. I mention a few collections of software where you can find most any program, but if you need help locating a particular type of software, Chapter 16 explains how to use a search service.

You then learn the mechanics of the downloading process. This discussion focuses on downloading software from Web sites because that's becoming the most common method of obtaining software. However, there are also enormous repositories of software stored at *FTP sites.* (In fact, many download links on Web pages actually point to software stored at FTP sites.) You'll learn what FTP is and how to download files directly from FTP sites in Chapter 12; the process is almost identical to downloading files through a Web site.

Finally, you learn what to *do* with a downloaded program once it's sitting on your disk. You can't actually use a program until you install it properly, but people often get stuck at this step because it is rarely described explicitly.

What Kinds of Programs Can I Download?

Every kind of program imaginable is on the Internet, including utilities, games, business software, home and hobby programs, and educational software. While some of it is commercial software, which often comes with a high price tag, most of it is freeware or low-cost shareware. This section mentions some reasons for downloading software, describes some Internet-related software you might want to get, and defines a few key terms.

 Downloading is a convenient way to get upgrades of your favorite programs, including new versions of your browser. If you have a program you love dearly, check the vendor's Web site frequently to stay informed about upgrades. Vendors like to distribute upgrades (and bug fixes) via the Internet because they don't have to pay packaging and shipping charges.

 Many developers let you download *beta* versions of their programs for free. Beta software is still in the development stage, which means that it is usually fairly functional, but often contains bugs. Like trial versions of shareware, betas are often time-sensitive. Users benefit from using betas because they get a peek at new software, and developers benefit because they get feedback and bug reports from the users. You can usually download beta versions of the Netscape Navigator browser from Netscape's Web site at http://home.netscape.com.

 Freeware is, as its name implies, completely free. A software author may choose to distribute his program as freeware in order to develop a user base, or just because he's good-natured and hopes others will find his program useful.

2 Beginning with Netscape Navigator 2.0, you can extend Navigator's capabilities with plug-ins. The most common type of plug-in tells Netscape how to display or play multimedia objects, such as movies, video, sound, and 3-D animation. Many companies are producing plug-ins and making them available on the Web. Currently, Netscape and Internet Explorer are the only browsers that support plug-ins.

3 Most plug-ins are so tightly integrated with Netscape that once they are installed, they work automatically within Netscape, loading in Netscape windows, and require no action from you. Netscape sometimes refers to the plug-ins that are automatically included in Netscape Navigator as *components*. (Chapter 7 discusses two of these components, LiveAudio and LiveVideo.) The term *plug-in* is currently in vogue, so many companies use it to refer to programs that are actually helper applications. (See the next step.)

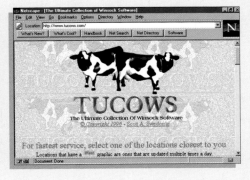

4 Like plug-ins, *helper applications* work with your browser to extend its capabilities. The difference between helper applications and plug-ins is that helper applications load as external programs that work outside Netscape, and you sometimes have to "manually" configure Netscape so that it knows how to use an application (see "How to Configure Helper Applications" in Chapter 7). The good news is that version 3.0 of Netscape recognizes most of the file types that previous versions needed helper applications to handle.

5 *Shareware* is software the author has made available to the public for a nominal fee. You can usually download free trial versions of these programs, and then register and pay for your copy only if you decide to keep using it. Software developers employ a variety of techniques to encourage users to "do the right thing" and pay for their programs. Some programs "die" after the trial period is over; others ship with all but the most basic features disabled and only become fully functional when you register the software.

How to Download a Program

As you may know, programs are comprised of dozens, if not hundreds, of individual files. When software developers want to make a program available for downloading, they compress all the component files into one large file, which they place on the Internet. Downloading is the process of copying this file onto your hard disk. On this page and the next, you'll see how to download and install a trial version of a shareware plug-in called EarthTime (http://www.starfishsoftware.com). This plug-in uses the Netscape window to display the current time in locations of your choice around the world.

System Requirements

- Windows 95 or Windows NT Workstation 3.51
- IBM PC 386 or 100% compatible (Recommended: IBM PC 486 or 100% compatible)
- 6 MB RAM
- 2 MB free hard disk space
- Mouse or other pointing device
- Using the plug-in requires Netscape Navigator 2.0 for Windows 95 or Windows NT
- Internet Time Synchronization is not available for Windows NT

▶ 1 Begin by reading any download and/or installation instructions at the site. This information is usually located on the same page as the link that actually downloads the file. Many sites list the hardware and operating-system requirements for the programs you can download and provide brief explanations of how each program works. It's a good idea to read this information carefully to confirm that the software will run on your system and that it does what you want it to do.

7 When the file transfer is completed, Netscape simply closes the Saving Location dialog box and leaves you on the same Web page. You can now close your Internet connection, close Netscape, and turn the page to learn how to install the software.

6 You can do other work on your computer while a file is being transferred, but the download may take longer, because the computer has to share its resources with the other programs you're using.

2 Once you've decided to go ahead with the download, follow links until you get to the one that actually initiates the download. This link is frequently the word *download*, but it can vary. Click on the download link, and then go to step 3 if you see the Unknown File Type dialog box, or to step 4 if you see the Save As dialog box. If you're downloading a file with the .zip extension and you have WinZip version 6.1 on your computer, the WinZip Wizard might (depending on your setup) automatically download the ZIP file, extract its compnent files, and install the software for you. If this happens, you should skip to step 5 on the next page.

3 If the file you're downloading has an extension that Netscape doesn't recognize, it displays the Unknown File Type dialog box to inform you that it doesn't know what to do with the file. Because you want to download the file, click on the Save File button.

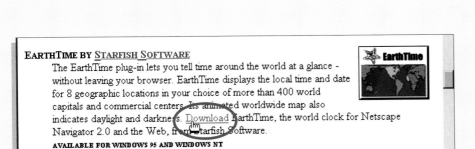

5 Netscape displays the Saving Location dialog box, just as it does when you save individual Web pages. This dialog box gives you a rough estimate of how much time the download will take.

4 The browser displays the Save As dialog box when it is about to download the software. Leave the file name as is, and choose a temporary folder in the Save In drop-down list. If you download software or other files frequently, it's a good idea to create a folder named TEMP or DOWNLOAD just for storing files you get from the Internet. Click on OK to start transferring the file.

How to Install a Program That You Have Downloaded

If you haven't already done so, use the instructions on the preceding page to download the program into a temporary folder on your hard disk. Then close all open programs before following these steps to install the software on your computer.

▶ **1** If the file you downloaded has a .zip extension, use WinZip to extract the setup files into the same temporary folder, and then go to step 4. (If you're not familiar with WinZip, see the tip on this page.)

▶ **WinZip is a shareware program for creating and opening files compressed in the ZIP format. It is a must-have if you frequently download files from the Internet or send documents via e-mail. WinZip is available at http://www.winzip.com. For help using WinZip, see Chapter 9.**

▶ **If you try out a program you've downloaded and decided you don't like it, it's best to uninstall it so that it doesn't waste disk space. Click on the Start button, point to Settings, and click on Control Panel. Double-click on Add/Remove Programs, select the program name in the Install/ Uninstall tab, and click on the Add/Remove button. If you don't see the program name listed in this dialog box, click on the Cancel button and look for a file in the program folder called uninstall.exe. Double-click on this file and follow the instructions.**

 Here is the newly installed EarthTime plug-in running in the Netscape Navigator window.

2 Most program files that you download—including the one shown here—have an .exe extension. Double-click on the EXE file to see what happens. Some EXEs automatically extract the files they contain and then launch the installation procedure. If you see a message about starting setup or installation, you have an EXE of this type, and you can skip to step 5. Otherwise, go to the next step.

3 Double-clicking on the EXE may extract the files without starting the setup program. This type of EXE usually uses a DOS-based extraction program, so after you double-click on the file, you might see an MS-DOS window as the files are being extracted. When the extraction is complete, you'll see the word *Finished* in the title bar of the MS-DOS window. Click on the Close button in the upper-right corner of the window to close it.

4 The extracted files will most likely appear in the same folder as the original file. (If you unzipped a ZIP file, the extracted files should also be in this same folder.) Look for a file called Setup.exe or Install.exe, and double-click on it to start the installation process.

6 When the installation is complete, you can start the new program by clicking on the program name in the Programs menu (click on the Start button, point to Programs, and then click on the program name), by double-clicking on the program icon in the folder that holds the program, or by double-clicking on a shortcut icon for the program on the desktop, as shown here.

5 Follow the onscreen prompts to complete the installation. The questions you have to answer will vary depending on the program you're installing. As part of the installation, most programs create a new folder and install themselves into it. As a final step, you will probably be asked to restart Windows.

CHAPTER 7

Using Plug-Ins and Helper Applications

Although your browser is perfectly adequate for most strolls around the Internet, sooner or later you may want to enhance its capabilities with plug-ins and helper applications. In this chapter, you learn how to use three programs that come with Netscape 3.0, and you find out how to configure Netscape to use third-party programs.

First, you learn about LiveAudio and LiveVideo, Netscape 3.0's plug-ins for playing sound and video files. These programs are so well integrated into Netscape Navigator that they don't seem like separate pieces of software. (You have to have a sound card and speakers to play sound files.)

Next, you learn how to use a Netscape 3.0 helper application called CoolTalk. If you have a microphone, a sound card, and speakers, CoolTalk lets you carry on a voice conversation with another CoolTalk user anywhere in the world using your Internet connection (without paying for long distance phone charges).

CoolTalk also has a *white board*—a blank window with a few drawing and typing tools that both participants in a CoolTalk session can see. As you talk on the "phone," you can place images on the white board for the other person to view, and you can use the drawing and typing tools to mark up the images as you would draw on an overhead transparency. All changes to the white board contents are simultaneously displayed on the other person's screen.

Finally, you learn how to configure third-party helper applications and plug-ins. Netscape doesn't automatically configure itself to use some of these programs, so you have to tell Netscape what types of files you want the program to handle.

How to Play Sound and Video Files

An increasing number of Web sites contain links to sound and video files. When you click on a link for one of these files, Netscape's LiveAudio or LiveVideo downloads the file from the Web site and plays it for you. LiveAudio can play sound files in all the common formats: AU, AIFF, MIDI, and WAV. Currently, LiveVideo can only play videos in the AVI format, so if you want to play MOV, MPG, or QT files (three other common video formats) you'll need to download a third-party program (see the Tip Sheet).

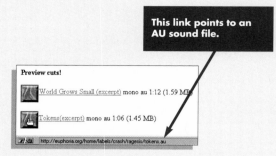

This link points to an AU sound file.

▶ **1** Many links to sound files indicate the size and format of the file. If the format isn't listed in the Web page itself, you can find out what it is by pointing to the link and looking at the URL in the status bar. To play the sound file, just click on the link.

8 The quality of video displayed on computer screens is still quite poor—the images are usually not very clear, and movements are often jerky. If you are particularly interested in video, you might want to experiment with third-party software for viewing video files. Companies are working hard to improve video quality, and new software is emerging all the time.

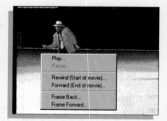

7 You can also right-click on the video to display a context menu with commands for manipulating the video. When you are finished viewing the video, close the Netscape window by clicking on its Close button.

TIP SHEET

▶ Visit http://www.windows95.com/apps/webplug.html to see an extensive collection of links to shareware plug-ins and helper applications. The list contains several programs that let you view videos and movies in formats other than AVI.

▶ Netscape 3.0 comes with another plug-in, Live3D, that lets you view Web sites that use VRML (Virtual Reality Markup Language) to create 3D worlds. Unfortunately, the huge amount of processing required makes it a frustrating experience to view even fairly simply VRML sites with anything slower than a fast 486.

▶ Some helper applications play *streaming* (or *real-time*) audio and video. That is, the software starts to play the file as it is being downloaded, instead of downloading the entire file first. In the Try It exercise that follows this chapter, you'll download and install a program called RealAudio, which lets you play sound files in the RealAudio (RA) format in real time.

2 After you click on the link, LiveAudio displays a small Netscape window and temporarily fills the window with Netscape's logo as the file is being downloaded. It can take anywhere from a few seconds to several minutes or longer to download a sound file, depending on the size of the file, the speed of your modem, and available bandwidth. (In some Web pages, the Netscape logo and the control panel shown in step 3 display directly in the page instead of in a separate window, as shown here.)

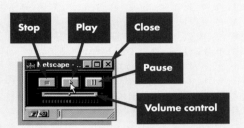

3 As soon as the file is downloaded, a simple control panel replaces the Netscape logo. Click the Play button to start playing the file. You can pause or stop the file at any time with the Pause and Stop buttons, and you can adjust the volume by dragging the marker on the volume control.

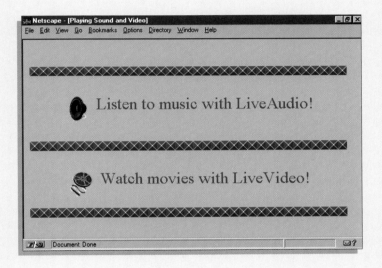

4 When you're done listening to the file, click on the Close button (the X) in the upper-right corner to close the window.

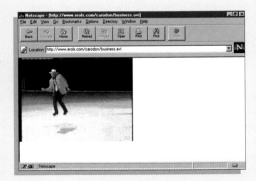

6 LiveVideo opens a new Netscape window and downloads the file. This is a good time to get a cup of coffee—downloading video files can try your patience. As soon as the file is downloaded, the first frame of the video appears in the upper-left corner of the window. Click on the image to play the video.

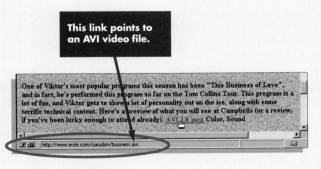

This link points to an AVI video file.

5 To view an AVI video file, click on the link. Like links to sound files, most links to video files list the file format, but you can also point to the link and check the URL in the status bar.

How to Use CoolTalk's Phone

Internet phone software such as CoolTalk has immense appeal, since it allows you to carry on long-distance "phone" conversations without incurring long-distance charges. This type of software is fairly new, so it still has some kinks, and the sound quality is not up to snuff. Nonetheless, it's so potentially useful that it's likely to take off soon.

 ❶ Connect to your ISP, and double-click on the CoolTalk shortcut icon in the Navigator folder to launch the program. You don't have to have Netscape open to use CoolTalk.

Drag to adjust silence level.

Click to adjust record and playback levels.

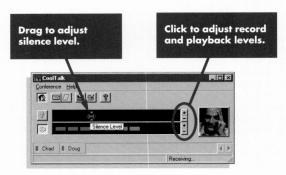

❽ The *silence level* tells CoolTalk not to send audio lower than the indicated level. You can adjust the level by dragging the two red triangles in the upper bar. Position the silence level just above the level of the record meter when you are not speaking to prevent CoolTalk from sending background noise to the other person. You can also use the plus and minus buttons to increase or decrease the record and playback levels. When you're ready to disconnect, click on the Start/Leave Conference button and click on Yes.

❼ If you want to read the person's business card, click on his or her photograph (or the default button showing the CoolTalk logo if there is no photograph) to display the About box. The Participant tab contains the person's business card. Additional tabs include information about the other person's computer.

TIP SHEET

▶ **When you install Netscape Navigator 3.0, it asks if you want to install CoolTalk. If you answer yes, it asks whether you want to install the CoolTalk Watchdog. Watchdog loads every time you turn on your computer, and launches CoolTalk whenever an invitation comes in.**

▶ **The sound quality of phone conversations is better if your sound card is full-duplex rather than half-duplex, because full-duplex cards can carry both voices in a conversation simultaneously, while half-duplex cards force you to "take turns." To check what kind of sound card you have, choose Conference, Options, click on the Audio tab, and check the Operation Mode setting. If you have a half-duplex sound card, you can ask the manufacturer whether you can upgrade it to full-duplex.**

▶ **In future versions of CoolTalk, you'll be able to use the Address Book to place calls to people with dynamically assigned IP addresses as well as to people with static IP addresses.**

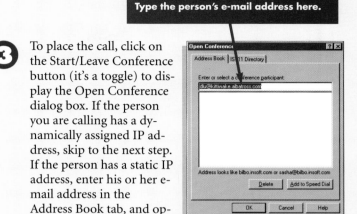

Type the person's e-mail address here.

2 The first time you load CoolTalk, it starts the Setup Wizard. (You can also start the wizard by choosing Setup Wizard from the CoolTalk Help menu.) The wizard tests your sound card and microphone, and then presents a "business card" in which you enter the personal data that CoolTalk sends to the person you talk with. (You can edit the card by choosing Conference, Options, and clicking on the Business Card tab.) When you're done filling in the information requested by the wizard, click on the Finish button. The person you want to talk to has to have CoolTalk or the CoolTalk Watchdog (see the Tip Sheet) running.

3 To place the call, click on the Start/Leave Conference button (it's a toggle) to display the Open Conference dialog box. If the person you are calling has a dynamically assigned IP address, skip to the next step. If the person has a static IP address, enter his or her e-mail address in the Address Book tab, and optionally click on the Add to Speed Dial button to create a Speed Dial button for the person. Then skip to step 5. (Check in Chapter 4 if you can't remember what IP addresses are all about.)

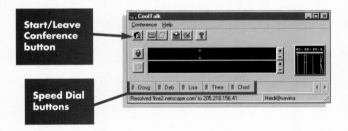

Start/Leave Conference button

Speed Dial buttons

4 If the person has a dynamically assigned IP address, you can't store the entry in the Address Book because the IP address changes each time the person connects to the Internet. Instead, you need to use the 411 directory, a database of currently connected CoolTalk users. The IP addresses in this directory are always current, including those that are dynamically assigned. To use the 411 directory, click on the 411 Directory tab and select the person's name from the list.

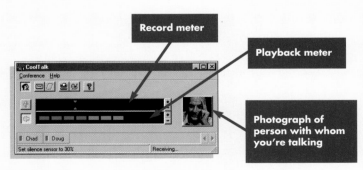

Record meter

Playback meter

Photograph of person with whom you're talking

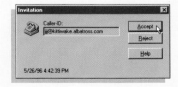

6 When you're connected, the Start/Leave Conference button looks pushed in. If the person with whom you're talking specified a scanned photograph in his or her business card, it is displayed in the CoolTalk window. Now you can begin your conversation. As you talk, the record meter on the upper black bar shows your voice levels, and the playback meter on the lower bar shows the voice levels of the other person.

5 Once you've selected the person's name in the Address Book or 411 Directory tab, click on OK to invite the person to talk. If you are at the receiving end, you'll see an Invitation message box. Click on Accept to establish the connection.

How to Use CoolTalk's White Board

CoolTalk's white board creates the illusion that you're in the same room with the other conference participants. As you're talking on CoolTalk's phone, you can sketch, write, or post ideas under discussion on your white board, and the white board on the other participant's screen is instantly updated. Either person can add, remove, or edit the white board's contents, making it a great tool for long-distance collaborations. You can also use it to make graphical presentations to remote clients.

TIP SHEET

▶ **In step 7, you can use the Capture, Desktop command to capture a picture of the entire Windows 95 desktop, or the Capture, Region command to capture a specific region of your screen. Then in step 8, click anywhere on the desktop if you chose the Desktop command, or drag with your mouse to outline a rectangular region if you chose Region, and click in the White Board window where you want to position the upper-left corner of the image.**

▶ **To clear the white board of drawing marks and text you've typed, choose Edit, Clear Markups. To clear it completely, choose Edit, Clear White Board.**

▶ **CoolTalk comes with a chat tool that lets you type messages back and forth in real time or display text-only documents. To use this tool, click on the Chat Tool button in the CoolTalk toolbar. This feature is somewhat awkward, because you can't see what the other person is typing until he or she "sends it." Another way to chat in writing is for each person to type on one half of the white board. If you use this technique, the other person's text appears in real time.**

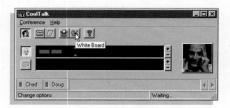

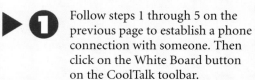

▶ **①** Follow steps 1 through 5 on the previous page to establish a phone connection with someone. Then click on the White Board button on the CoolTalk toolbar.

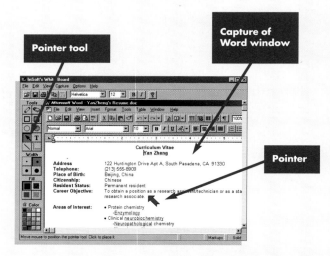

② The white board temporarily hides itself to let you view the other window. Click on the window's title bar to capture the entire window, or click in the middle of the window to capture just its contents. As soon as you click, the white board reappears. Click where you want the upper-left corner of the image to go. (The large arrow in this example is a pointer you can use to draw people's attention to particular areas of the white board. You display it by using the Pointer tool.)

⑦ To display a nongraphic file such as a word processing document or spreadsheet, open the file in the appropriate program (Word or Excel, for example), and then switch back to the white board by clicking on its taskbar button. Choose Capture, Window.

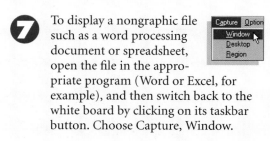

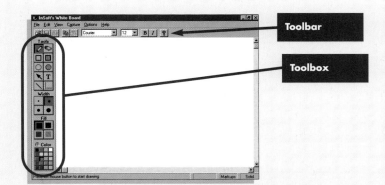

2 CoolTalk displays the White Board window. The toolbox along the left edge of the window contains drawing and text tools, and the toolbar at the top of the window contains buttons for standard operations such as saving, printing, cutting and pasting, and font formatting.

3 To open a graphic image into the white board, click on the Open toolbar button (the leftmost button). In the Open dialog box, select the desired graphic format from the Files of Type list, click on the file name, and then click on the Open button.

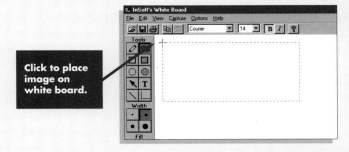

4 The mouse pointer takes on the shape of a clock as the image is loading. When the pointer becomes a crosshair, click where you want the upper-left corner of the image to go.

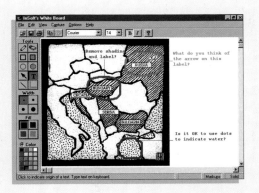

5 The image is displayed in the white board. If you want to draw on or around the image, select the desired drawing tool from the toolbox, and optionally change the default width, fill, and color for the selected tool. Then drag with your mouse to draw. This example shows an outline drawn with the Freehand Line tool. You can erase anything you've drawn (or typed) with the Eraser tool.

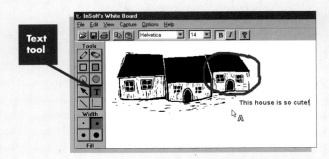

6 To type on the white board, click on the Text tool (the letter *A* gets attached to your mouse pointer) and optionally change the font, font size, and font attributes. Then click to place the insertion point, and type your text. Pressing Enter starts a new line directly under the first line.

Configuring Netscape to Use Third-Party Helper Applications and Plug-Ins

S ome third-party helper applications and plug-ins automatically tell Netscape how they should be used. With other programs, however, you need to supply this information to Netscape yourself; specifically, you need to tell Netscape what types of files the helper can handle. There are two ways to do this. One is to enter all the information in the Helpers tab of the Preferences dialog box (see the Tip Sheet). An easier method, and the one shown here, is to first download and install the helper application, and then wait until the first time Netscape encounters a file of the type you want the program to handle. At that point, you can configure Netscape to use the helper application "on the fly."

▶ **1** If you haven't yet done so, download and install the helper application or plug-in. Most sites that contain files that need to be handled by a helper application or plug-in tell you what software is required and provide a link to a site where you can download it. In this example, taken from the PBS Web site, they tell you that you need a plug-in called VDOLive to view the video clips available at the site.

7 Netscape launches the program you selected and plays the file whose link you clicked on earlier. In the future, Netscape will automatically use the same third-party software to handle any files with the same extension as the one you just viewed.

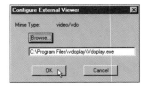

6 Netscape displays the path and file name in the Configure External Viewer dialog box. Click on the OK button.

TIP SHEET

▶ **If you prefer, you can configure Netscape to use a helper application or plug-in by entering the information in the Preferences dialog box. Choose Options, General Preferences, and click on the Helpers tab. Click on the Help button in the lower-right corner of the dialog box if you need assistance.**

▶ **If you choose Help, About Plug-ins, Netscape displays detailed information about all the helper applications and plug-ins you are using.**

Click on a link for the type of file you want the third-party program to handle. In this example, the link points to a file with the .vdo extension. VDO files are video files that have to be played with the VDOLive video player (available at http://www.vdo.com).

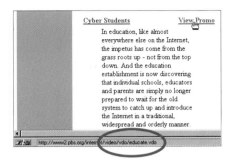

If Netscape already knows about the program, it launches the program automatically. If it doesn't, it throws up its hands and displays the Unknown File Type dialog box to tell you it doesn't know what to do with the file. Click on the Pick App button to pick the application you want to handle the file.

HEY...COULD YOU GIVE ME A HAND WITH THIS FILE?

SURE.

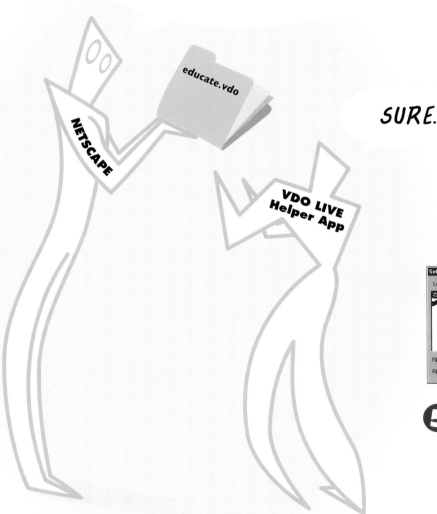

In the Configure External Viewer dialog box, click on the Browse button to find the executable file that launches the third-party software.

Look for the file in the folder that contains the program, the vdoplay folder in this example. The file will have an extension of .exe and its name will likely be the name of the program itself. Here, the executable file that runs the VDOLive player is Vdoplay.exe. When you find the EXE file, click on it, and then click on the Open button.

Here's a chance to practice what you've learned in the first seven chapters of this book. In this exercise, you'll download, install, and try out a helper application called RealAudio. RealAudio plays *streaming* sound files, meaning that it plays files as they are being transmitted, so you don't have to wait for slow downloads. You need to have at least a 486/66 DX computer and a 28.8 modem to use RealAudio 2.0, the version downloaded in this exercise. Also keep in mind that Web sites change frequently, so the Web pages and links you see may differ slightly from the ones shown here.

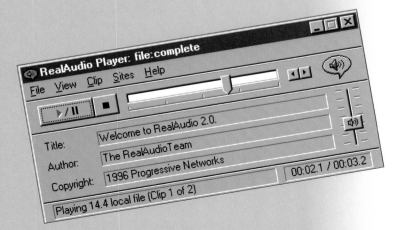

 1

Double-click on the Netscape Navigator icon to start Netscape.

 2

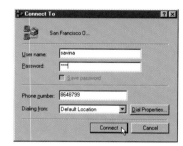

In the Connect To dialog box that appears, type your password, and click on the Connect button.

 3

After the Netscape Navigator window appears, click in the Location text box to select the current URL. (The URL on your screen is probably different than the one shown here.)

 4

Type the URL for RealAudio's Web site, http://www. realaudio. com. Then press Enter to connect to the site.

 5

Choose Bookmarks, Add Bookmark (or press Ctrl+D) to bookmark the RealAudio site so that you can easily return to it later.

6

Click on the RealAudio Player link on the RealAudio home page.

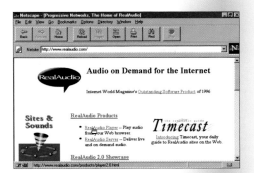

7

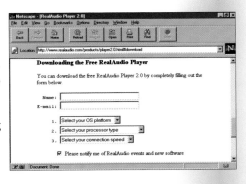

Click on the link for downloading the free version of RealAudio 2.0 (or later). (If you find this software useful, you might want to return to RealAudio's Web site and buy the Standard Edition on CD, which includes documentation, tech support, and a few other goodies.)

8

RealAudio displays a form to gather information about your operating system and hardware.

9

Fill in the Name and E-mail text boxes, and make the appropriate choices in the three drop-down lists. Then click on the button labeled Go to Download and Instructions Page.

10

Scroll down and read the download and installation instructions.

Download and installation instructions:
Click on the link above to begin downloading. Locate and launch the file you downloaded by exploring your hard drive or choosing the Run option in the Start menu. (The file is where your Web browser saved it.) This will begin the RealAudio setup process. Then read the RealAudio Help & FAQ for the RealAudio Player 2.0 release notes.

Important notice regarding your CPU:
In order to use the new music algorithm of RealAudio 2.0, you need at least a 486/66 DX (Windows) or a 68040/25 with FPU (Macintosh). However, you will be able to take advantage of all other RealAudio 2.0 features.

Your selections were:

Product: RealAudio Player 2.0
Platform: Windows 95
CPU Speed: 486
Connection: 28.8 kbps dialup

To make changes to your selections please use the back button in your Web browser.

11

RealAudio Player 2.01 for Microsoft Windows 95

Click here to download from site 1
(best for North America East Coast and European users)

Click here to download from site 2
(best for North America West Coast and other international users)

Scroll back up to the top of the page and click on the appropriate download site.

Continue to next page ▶

TRY IT!

Continue below

12

Netscape displays the Save As dialog box to ask where to store the file on your disk. Keep the default file name, select a folder in the Save In drop-down list, and click on the Save button to start the download.

13

You'll see the Saving Location dialog box as the file is downloaded.

14

When the Saving Location dialog box disappears, click on the taskbar button for your ISP connection, and then click on the Disconnect button.

15

Click on the Close button in the Netscape window to close the program.

16

Now you're ready to install RealAudio. Display the folder that contains the downloaded file, and double-click on the file to start the installation.

17

RealAudio extracts all the installation files automatically, and presents you with the first Setup message box. (Just click on Accept if you see a licensing agreement dialog box.) Enter your name and optionally the name of your company, and then click on Continue.

18

RealAudio confirms the information you entered. Click on OK to continue with the setup.

19

In the next dialog box, select your modem speed from the drop-down list, and click on OK.

20

Choose Express Setup to install RealAudio with all the default settings.

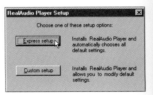

21

RealAudio displays a message telling you that the program has been successfully installed. Click on the OK button.

22

Next, RealAudio displays its program window and plays a short welcome message. After the message ends, click on the Close button. The program is now set up on your computer. Because this helper application automatically configures Netscape to work with it, you can now connect to a Web site that uses RealAudio, and take it for a spin.

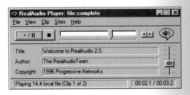

23

Start Netscape and connect to your ISP again. Then click on the current URL in the Location text box, and type the URL for National Public Radio, **http://www.npr.org**. Press Enter to connect to NPR, and then click on the link for the current day's newscast. You may need to hunt for another link in the (not unlikely) event that NPR's site changes.

24

Click on the link to transmit the newscast in RealAudio 2.0 format. (Some links may be labeled [Soundfile].)

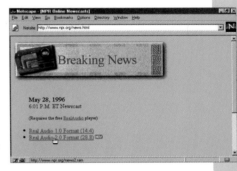

25

After a moment, the RealAudio window pops up and begins playing the newscast. You can adjust the volume with the volume control on the right. When you've finished listening to the broadcast, click on the Close button to close the RealAudio window. Many sites use RealAudio, so you will have ample opportunity to use this helper application.

CHAPTER 8

Communicating with E-mail

For many people, e-mail is the best part of using the Internet. E-mail has several advantages over the telephone: You can easily retain records of your communications, you can avoid long-distance phone charges, and you can send messages at any time of day or night without worrying about business hours and time zones. (E-mail is good for friendships too. If you come up with a brilliant inspiration at 2:00 A.M., you can tell your best buddy about it right then without disrupting anyone's sleep.)

In this chapter, you first learn how to send and receive e-mail messages. Next, you learn how to reply to a message and how to forward a message to someone else. Finally, you learn how to use an address book to store e-mail addresses so that you don't have to memorize them or type them over and over.

The examples in this chapter use Netscape Mail, the e-mail program integrated into Netscape Navigator starting with version 2.0. Netscape Mail is convenient because it lets you handle e-mail from within your browser. Several other e-mail programs for direct Internet connections run separately from your browser. The most popular one is called Eudora (available at http://www.qualcomm.com). All e-mail programs work in pretty much the same way, so the concepts discussed in this chapter apply to programs other than Netscape Mail.

Before you try the features described in this chapter, make sure you have entered the names of your ISP's incoming and outgoing mail servers in the Servers tab of Netscape's Preferences dialog box (choose Options, Mail and News Preferences). Refer to "Installing and Configuring Netscape" in Chapter 4 if you need help with this.

How to Send an E-Mail Message

Writing and sending an e-mail message is very straightforward: You type the e-mail address of the recipient, the subject line, and the body of the message, and then you click on the Send button. That's all there is to it. The steps on this page describe sending e-mail when you're connected to your ISP, but you can also compose messages offline, and then send them the next time you're connected. (See the Tip Sheet.)

TIP SHEET

▶ **If you want to see what messages you've sent out, you can double-click on the Sent folder in the Mail Folder pane of the Netscape Mail window. You'll learn about the various panes in the Netscape Mail window on the next page.**

▶ **You can easily switch from Netscape Mail back to the main Netscape window by clicking on Netscape's taskbar button.**

▶ **If you want to compose a message while you are not connected to your ISP, choose Options, Deferred Delivery in the Message Composition window. Then follow the steps on this page to write your message. When you click on the Send button, Netscape places a copy of the message in the Outbox folder. The next time you're connected, choose File, Send Messages in Outbox to send the message. (Remember to change back to Options, Immediate Delivery to send messages while you are online.)**

▶ **1** Click on the Mail icon in the lower-right corner of the Netscape window (or choose Window, Netscape Mail).

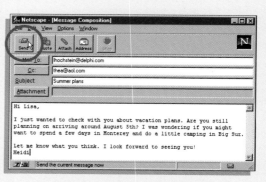

8 Type the body of the message, and then click on the Send button. After Netscape sends the message, it automatically closes the Message Composition window. If you are finished using e-mail, close the Netscape Mail window by clicking on its Close button.

7 If you wish, use the Attachment button to specify one or more attachments—either files or Web pages—to send with the message. (You'll learn about sending and receiving attachments in the next chapter.)

2 Netscape prompts you for your mail password, which is usually the same as the password you use to connect to your ISP. Type the password and click on OK. (To avoid entering the password in the future, choose Options, Mail and News Preferences, click on the Organization tab, mark the Remember Mail Password check box, and then click on OK.)

3 Netscape displays the Netscape Mail window. Click on the To:Mail toolbar button to display the Message Composition window. (You can also display the Message Composition window from the main Netscape window by choosing File, New Mail Message or by pressing Ctrl+M.)

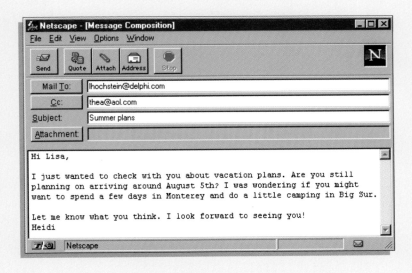

4 Type the recipient's e-mail address in the Mail To text box. To send the message to several people, type all their e-mail addresses separated by commas. If you use Netscape's address book, you can save yourself some typing by clicking on the Mail To button (or the Address toolbar button) and selecting the recipient from the Select Addresses dialog box. (See "How to Store E-Mail Addresses" later in this chapter.)

5 If you want to send copies of this message to one or more people, type the e-mail addresses in the Cc text box. If you want to send blind copies, choose View, Mail Bcc to add the Bcc text box to the Message Composition window, and then type the e-mail addresses in the Bcc text box. (Mail To and Cc recipients won't see the names of Bcc recipients. Bcc recipients will see the names of the Mail To and Cc recipients, but they won't see the names of the other people to whom you sent blind copies.)

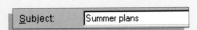

6 Type a subject for the message in the Subject text box. The subject will appear in the recipient's e-mail inbox next to your name and/or e-mail address.

How to Handle E-Mail Messages You Receive

Netscape checks your ISP's incoming mail server for new e-mail messages at ten-minute intervals while you are connected, and it alerts you when new messages are waiting. (You can change how frequently Netscape checks mail. Choose Options, Mail and News Preferences, and click on the Servers tab.) When you tell Netscape to retrieve the messages, it downloads them to your Inbox folder. Once you've read the messages, you can leave them in your inbox indefinitely if you want. But you'll have an easier time handling your e-mail if you periodically do some housecleaning, deleting messages you don't need, and moving those you do into other folders for safekeeping and convenient access.

TIP SHEET

▶ **You can resize the panes in the Netscape Mail window by dragging the gray borders that separate them.**

▶ **You can delete several messages at a time by selecting all the messages before pressing the Delete key. To select adjacent messages, click on the first message, and then Shift+click on the last message. To select nonadjacent messages, click on the first one, and then Ctrl+click on all the additional messages.**

▶ **By default, Netscape sorts messages according to date. To change the sort order, click on the gray buttons at the top of the Message Header pane. For example, to sort in alphabetical order by sender, click on the Sender button.**

▶ **If your Inbox folder contains a lot of messages, you may want to flag the important ones so that you can come back to them easily. To do this, click in the column to the right of the Sender name in the Message Header pane to place a small red flag in the message header. You can jump between flagged messages by choosing the First Flagged, Next Flagged, and Previous Flagged in the Go menu.**

▶ **❶** When new messages are waiting on your ISP's mail server, Netscape places an exclamation point next to the Mail icon in the lower-right corner of the Netscape window. Click on the icon to display the Netscape Mail window and retrieve the messages.

❽ To print a message, click on it in the Message Header pane, click on the Print toolbar button, then click on OK in the Print dialog box.

Mail Folder	Unread	Total	Sender			Subject	Date
📁 **Inbox**	**4**	**12**	📧	paul copeland	· ·	crying puppy	5/22/96 22...
📁 Outbox			📧	Andrea Holson	·	Thanks!	5/24/96 6:47
📁 Sent		43	📧	Stephanie Smith, P...	·	bloat in miniature poodles	5/24/96 9:14
📁 Trash		1	📧	Deborah Craig	·	Yo Heidi	5/26/96 5:50
📁 CD Orders		10	📧	DebACraig@aol.com	·	New Address	12:40
📁 Dog Chatter			📧	DebACraig@aol.com	✓ ✓	Doggie Daze	12:40
📁 Email		1	📧	**Doug Urner**	· ✓	**Re: Hi There**	**12:54**
📁 Mailing List Info		2	📧	**Doug Urner**	· ✓	**Poodles and Cows**	**12:57**
📁 Web Design		4	📧	**Doug Urner**	· ✓	**Vacation in August**	**12:58**
			📧	**Doug Urner**	· ✓	**Netscape addresses**	**13:09**

❼ The new folder appears in the Mail Folder pane. Drag the message from the Message Header pane and release the mouse when you're pointing to the folder. Netscape moves the message from the Inbox folder to your newly created folder.

2 As shown in the middle of this page, the Netscape Mail window is divided into three panes. The Message Header pane displays the sender, the subject, and the date of each message in the Inbox folder, which is located at the top of the Mail Folder pane. New messages are boldfaced and marked with a green flag.

New messages

Use the scroll bar to view the entire message.

3 To read a message, click on it in the Message Header pane. The message is displayed in the Message pane. You may have to use the vertical scroll bar to bring the entire message into view.

Mail Folder pane

Message Header pane

Message pane

4 To delete a message you've read, click on the message in the Message Header pane and click on the Delete toolbar button or press the Delete key. Netscape sends the message to the Trash folder. Until you empty the Trash folder—by choosing File, Empty Trash Folder—you can redisplay any of the messages it contains.

6 Type a name for the folder and click on OK.

5 If you want to store a message, first create a folder for it in the Mail Folder pane (if an appropriate folder doesn't already exist). To do this, choose File, New Folder. (Note that the folders in the Mail Folder pane are visible only in Netscape; they aren't actual folders in Windows 95. Netscape puts all the information about these folders in Netscape\Navigator\Mail, but you don't need to deal with these files directly.)

How to Reply to or Forward an E-Mail Message

Like other e-mail programs, Netscape Mail lets you *reply* to and *forward* messages. When you reply to a message, you don't have to re-type the person's e-mail address or the subject line, because Netscape fills in the information for you. The forward feature lets you pass a message you received on to someone else.

▶ **1** To reply to a message, start by clicking on the message in the Message Header pane. Then click on the Re:Mail toolbar button.

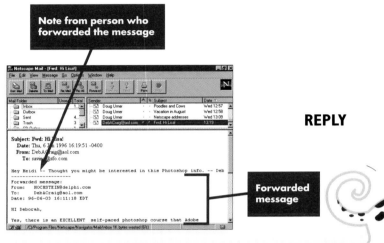

Note from person who forwarded the message

REPLY

Forwarded message

8 When you receive a forwarded message, the sender listed in the Message Header pane is the name of the person who forwarded the message. The body of the message includes any message added by the person forwarding the message, as well as the forwarded message itself.

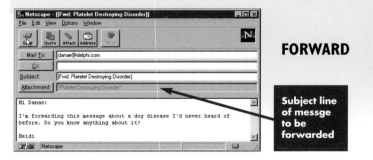

FORWARD

Subject line of messge to be forwarded

 7 Netscape opens the Message Composition window and inserts the subject line of the for-warded message in the Subject text box. It pre-cedes the subject with *Fwd:* and encloses the whole line within brackets. Type the recipient's e-mail address in the Mail To text box, and op-tionally type a brief message. (You won't see the content of the message being forwarded, but Netscape lists its subject in the Attachment box to indicate that it will be sent.) Then click on the Send button.

2 Netscape displays the Message Composition window with the sender's e-mail address already entered in the Mail To text box and the original subject entered in the Subject text box. Netscape prefaces the subject with *Re:* to let the recipient know that your message is a reply. (You can, of course, revise the subject if you wish.)

To: Spot
From: Bowser
Subject: Park

Wanna go?

To: Bowser
From: Spot
Subject: Re: Park

Yup!

3 Type your message, and then click on the Send button.

4 In e-mail correspondence, it is standard practice to quote portions of the original message in your reply. This lets the recipient know what parts of the original message you're responding to. To quote the original message, follow steps 1 and 2, and then click on the Quote toolbar button.

To: Max
From: Spot
Subject: Fwd: Warning

I got this from Bowser.
- - - - - - - - - - -
Warning! Leash law is now being enforced.

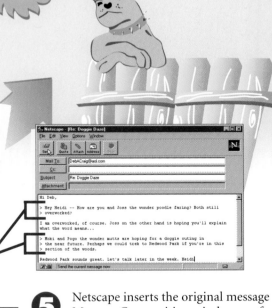

Quotations from original message

5 Netscape inserts the original message in the Message Composition window, prefacing each line with the > symbol. You can type your own text in between the lines of original text, and you can delete any portions of the original text you don't want. When you're done, click on the Send button.

6 To forward a message, click on the message you want to forward in the Message Header pane, and then click on the Forward button.

How to Store E-Mail Addresses

You can store e-mail addresses in Netscape's address book. Then when you're writing a message, you can simply select the e-mail address from the address book instead of typing it. The address book also lets you group people together in *lists*—you could create a list for your family members or for the members of your book club, for example. Then when you want to send a message to all the members of the list, you just enter the name of the list in the Mail To text box, and Netscape sends the message to everyone in the list.

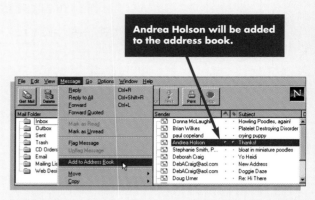

Andrea Holson will be added to the address book.

1 If you want to store the e-mail address of someone who sent you a message, click on the person's message in the Message Header pane of the Netscape Mail window, and then choose Message, Add to Address Book. This method is fast, but it doesn't let you store information other than the person's e-mail address. If you have several addresses to enter or if you want to enter more complete information about people, use the method described in steps 2 and 3.

If you type the person's nickname, Netscape replaces it with the full name and e-mail address.

8 If you entered a nickname for a person or list in step 3, then instead of using the Select Addresses dialog box, you can type the nickname in the Mail To text box. As soon as you press the Tab key or click in another part of the Mail Composition window, Netscape replaces the nickname with the name of the person or list, followed by the e-mail address or the full name of the list in brackets.

7 Click on the person or list you want, and click on the To button. If you're sending a message to multiple people, click on each address and then click on the To, Cc, or Bcc button to have Netscape place the addresses in the appropriate text boxes. (Remember that the Bcc text box is not displayed by default. If you want to use it, first choose View, Mail Bcc in the Message Composition window.) Then click on OK to close the dialog box.

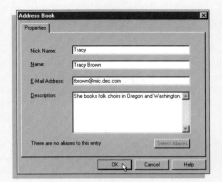

2 To enter e-mail addresses directly into the address book, start by choosing Window, Address Book. (This command is available in the main Netscape window, the Netscape Mail window, and the Message Composition window.) Netscape displays the Address Book window shown in the center of this page.

3 Choose Item, Add User, and then fill in the Nickname, Name, E-Mail Address, and Description text boxes. (Step 8 explains what nicknames are for. The description isn't used outside the address book.) Click on OK when you're done. Repeat this process to add more e-mail addresses to your address book. When you're finished, click on the Close button in the upper-right corner of the Address Book window.

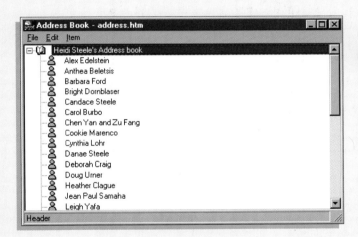

4 To create a list, start by choosing Item, Add List in the Address Book window. Select the default entry in the Name text box (New Folder) and replace it with the actual name of the list. Optionally enter a nickname and a description, and then click on OK.

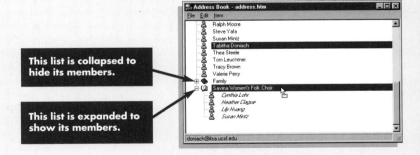

This list is collapsed to hide its members.

This list is expanded to show its members.

5 The new list is added to your address book. (Notice that Netscape uses book icons to indicate lists.) Now add e-mail addresses to the list by dragging and dropping them on the list name. Netscape leaves the e-mail addresses in their original locations in the address book, and creates *aliases* (displayed in italics) for the addresses in the list. Notice that you can click on the plus/minus sign next to each list to display or hide the individual addresses in the list. When you're finished creating the list, close the Address Book window.

Mail To:

6 To use the address book, click on the Mail To button (or the Address button) in the Message Composition window to display the Select Addresses dialog box.

CHAPTER 9

Sending and Receiving Documents with E-Mail

 E-mail is a wonderful way to communicate, but it has its limitations. The main drawback is that e-mail messages are text-only files (also known as *ASCII* files). Files that include anything other than plain text—word processing files, spreadsheets, graphics, program files, and so on—are known as *binary* files. If you want to send binary files, you have to send them as *attachments* to your messages.

But there is a catch: The Internet can't transmit binary files via e-mail unless they are first *encoded* as ASCII files. For many years, people used a pair of UNIX programs called uue ncode and uud ecode (or their Windows counterparts) to encode files before sending them, and to decode files after receiving them. In the last few years, a new standard called MIME (Multipurpose Internet Mail Extensions) has emerged that lets programs—including browsers—handle the encoding and decoding automatically. However, file-transfer technology is not yet completely standardized, so don't be surprised if you run into occasional snags.

As in the previous chapter, the examples in this chapter use Netscape Mail. You begin by learning how to attach one or two documents to an e-mail message, and how to download a document on the receiving end. Then you learn how to send a large number of files as a single attachment by *zipping* (compressing) the files into a single ZIP file, and you discover how to decompress a ZIP attachment at the receiving end. Finally, you learn two ways of attaching a URL to an e-mail message and viewing the Web page associated with an attached URL that you receive.

How to Attach a Document to an E-Mail Message

When you attach a document to an e-mail message, your browser sends an exact copy of the file to the recipient. At the receiving end, the recipient can open, edit, and print the file, just as if it had been created on his or her own computer. Before you attach a document to an e-mail message, make sure that the recipient has a program that can open the file. For example, if you send a Word for Windows document, the recipient needs to have Word for Windows or another word processing program that can handle Word files.

TIP SHEET

► If you add a file in the Attachments dialog box and then decide against attaching it, click on the file name, and then click on the Delete button. Netscape removes the file name from the Attachments dialog box. (It doesn't, however, delete the file from your disk.)

► Be careful about attaching files with file names that exceed eight characters if you are sending them to someone who will open them with a program designed to run under Windows 3.1. Windows 3.1 programs truncate long file names to eight characters, and this might make it difficult for the recipient to figure out what the files are.

► If you're sending a file to someone who uses a Mac, either save it in Mac format (if the program you used to create the file uses different formats for Mac and PC files) or make sure the recipient can handle a PC file. Sending a file over the Internet to a Mac computer does not automatically convert the file for use on a Mac.

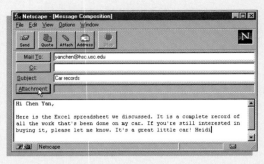

► **1** Display the Message Composition window (click on the To:Mail button in the Netscape Mail window or choose File, New Mail Message from the main Netscape window), fill in the Mail To, Cc, and Subject text boxes, and type a message if you want. Then click on the Attachment button (or click on the Attach toolbar button) to display the Attachments dialog box.

Netscape lists the attachments here.

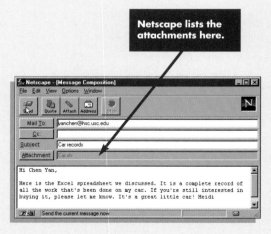

6 Netscape lists the name of the attached file in the Attachment box. (Since the Attachment box is gray, the file name will be hard to see.) Click on the Send button to send the e-mail message. Because Netscape has to send a copy of the attached file, the message will take longer to send than messages with no attachments, and obviously the larger the attachment, the longer the transfer time.

2 Click on the Attach File button to display the Enter File to Attach dialog box.

3 Use the Look In drop-down list to display the folder containing the document you want to attach, click on the file name, and then click on the Open button.

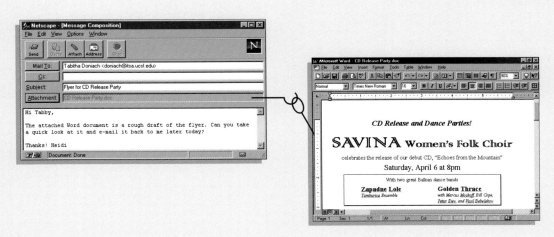

5 Leave the As Is option button selected, and then click on OK to return to the Message Composition window. (Choose the Convert to Plain Text option button only if you want to strip all the formatting from the attachment and send only plain text.)

4 Netscape displays the name of the file in the Attachments dialog box. If you want to add one or two more attachments, you can repeat steps 2 and 3 to add more file names to this dialog box. When you are sending many files, however, it is usually easier for the recipient if you use WinZip to compress the individual files into one ZIP file. That way, the recipient only has to handle one attached file. (See "How to Attach Multiple Documents with WinZip" later in this chapter.) Of course, if you're attaching pictures or charts to illustrate points in your e-mail message, it makes more sense to send each file as an individual attachment.

How to View and Save an Attached Document

Downloading a document attached to an e-mail message is much like downloading a document from a link in a Web page. You click on the link, tell Netscape where you want to put the file and what you want to name it, and then wait while Netscape saves the file. Because of the similarities, this discussion should be very familiar to those of you who practiced downloading programs in Chapter 6 and the first Try It!

▶ ❶ Click on the message in the Message Header pane of the Netscape Mail window.

▶ **The View menu in the Netscape Mail window contains the commands Attachments As Links and Attachments Inline. When Attachments Inline is selected, Netscape displays certain types of attachments directly in the Message pane, instead of displaying a link to the attachment. (If Netscape doesn't know how to display a file—this is true for most documents, including word processing and spreadsheet files—it displays it as a link even if Attachments Inline is selected.) The Attachments As Links command tells Netscape to display all attachments as links, regardless of their file types.**

▶ **When you click on an attachment link, Netscape responds differently depending on the attachment type. With most files, it displays the Save As dialog box to let you save the file to disk. However, it may also display some attachments inline. The way Netscape handles attachment links varies depending on the settings in the Helpers tab of the Preferences dialog box (displayed by choosing Options, General Preferences).**

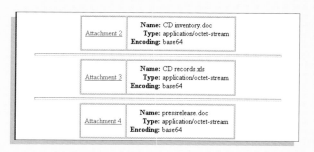

❻ You may receive messages that have multiple attachments. If you do, just repeat steps 2 through 4 to save each document.

❷ Scroll down to the end of the message in the Message pane. Netscape places the link for the attachment in a box that also supplies information about the attachment. The Name is simply the file name. Type lists the MIME type of the file, and Encoding lists the kind of encoding that was used. (You don't normally have to pay attention to the Type and Encoding information.) Click on the link to view or save the file.

❸ In most cases, Netscape displays the Save As dialog box. (See the Tip Sheet to learn about exceptions.) Choose a folder from the Save In drop-down list, and click on the Save button.

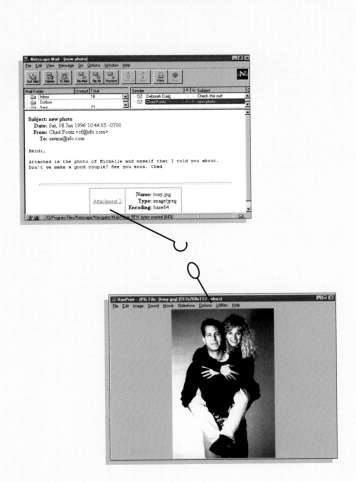

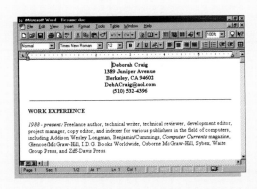

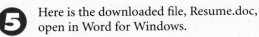

❹ Netscape saves the file to your disk. You can now double-click on the file to open it. Windows 95 opens the file using whatever program was used to create it, assuming you have the program on your disk. If you don't, you might be able to use a comparable program that recognizes the file type of the downloaded file.

❺ Here is the downloaded file, Resume.doc, open in Word for Windows.

How to Attach Multiple Documents with WinZip

The best method of sending a large number of files to someone via e-mail is to use a shareware program called WinZip. Using WinZip, you can compress the files into a single ZIP file (also called an *archive*) and attach the ZIP file to an e-mail message. If you haven't already done so, you need to download and install WinZip. (The program is available at http://www.winzip.com.) Make sure you download the most recent version designed for Windows 95. If you need help with this, refer to Chapter 6.

► **1** Start WinZip either by choosing it from the Start, Programs menu or by double-clicking on a shortcut to the program, as shown here.

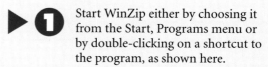

7 Now follow all the steps in "How to Attach a Document to an E-Mail Message" earlier in this chapter, selecting the ZIP file in step 3.

6 WinZip compresses the selected files. This process can take a few seconds to several minutes, depending on the number and size of the files. Once this batch of files is compressed, you can repeat steps 4 and 5 if necessary to add files from other folders. When you're done, click on the Close button in the upper-right corner of the WinZip window.

TIP SHEET

▶ **If WinZip started with the WinZip Wizard and you clicked on the WinZip Classic button (as described in step 2), when you close the program, WinZip asks you which interface you want to use the next time you start WinZip. Feel free to experiment with both the classic interface and the wizard to see which one you prefer.**

▶ **If you add a file to a WinZip archive and then decide you don't want to include it, click on the file name in the WinZip window, and press the Delete key. WinZip displays the Delete dialog box. Make sure the Selected Files option button is marked, and click on the delete button. This removes the file from the archive but does not delete it from your disk.**

2 If you see the WinZip Wizard (a feature added in version 6.1), click on the WinZip Classic button to display the standard WinZip window, and then click on the New button to display the New Archive dialog box.

3 Choose a location for the file in the Create In drop-down list, and type a name for the file in the File Name text box. (If you omit the .zip extension, WinZip adds it for you.) Then click on OK.

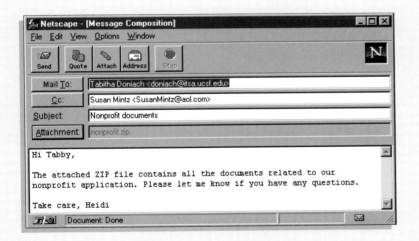

4 Click on the Add button to tell WinZip which files you want to compress.

5 WinZip displays the Add dialog box. First use the Add From drop-down list to select the folder that contains the files, and then select the desired files. To add a group of adjacent files, click on the first file in the group, and Shift+click on the last file. To add nonadjacent files, click on the first one, and then Ctrl+click on each additional file. When all the files are selected, click on the Add button.

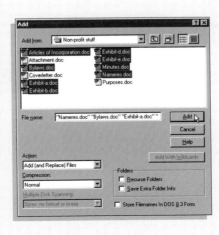

How to Save and Unzip an Attached ZIP File

S aving an attached ZIP file can be a little different than saving other attached files, because depending on your Netscape configuration, WinZip may or may not start running as soon as you click on a link to a ZIP file. But regardless of your setup, saving and unzipping an attachment is quick and easy. If you haven't already done so, you need to download and install the most recent Windows 95 version of WinZip (see Chapter 6 for help). The program is available at http://www.winzip.com.

TIP SHEET

▶ **If you want Netscape to launch WinZip automatically when you click on a link for a ZIP file, and it is not currently configured to do so, choose Options, General Preferences, and click on the Helpers tab. Click on the line for application/x-zip-compressed, and click on the Launch the Application option button at the bottom of the dialog box. Next, click on the Browse button, and in the Select an Appropriate Viewer dialog box, find and click on the executable file for WinZip, Winzip32.exe (it should be in the WinZip folder). Click on the Open button, and then click on OK to close the Preferences dialog box.**

▶ **The compression program most widely used on a Mac is a shareware program called StuffIt. If you want to exchange compressed files with a Mac user, either you'll need to get the PC version of StuffIt, or the Mac user will have to get a compression program that can handle ZIP files.**

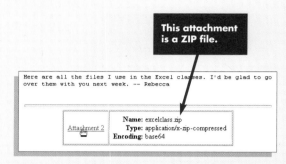

This attachment is a ZIP file.

Here are all the files I use in the Excel classes. I'd be glad to go over them with you next week. -- Rebecca

Attachment 2   **Name:** excelclass.zip
                Type: application/x-zip-compressed
                Encoding: base64

▶ **1** Click on the message that contains the ZIP attachment, and then scroll to the bottom of the message and click on the attachment link.

8 Depending on the number and size of the files you're extracting, it can take a few seconds to several minutes to extract them. WinZip shows you its progress at the bottom of the WinZip window. When it's finished, click on the Close button in the upper-right corner of the window to close the program.

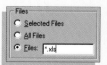

7 The Files option button in the Extract dialog box allows you to extract only files that match the criteria you type in the text box. In this example, *.xls will extract only the Excel spreadsheet files, (bonus*.* would extract only files whose names begin with *bonus*, and so on).

2 If you see the Viewing Location message box, Netscape is configured to start WinZip automatically whenever you click on a link to a ZIP file, and you can skip directly to step 4.

3 If you see the Save As dialog box, Netscape is not configured to start WinZip automatically when it encounters a ZIP file, so you need to "manually" save the file. Pick a folder for the ZIP file in the Save In drop-down list, keep the existing file name, and click on the Save button. Once the file is saved, double-click on the file to start WinZip.

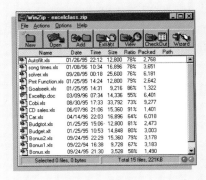

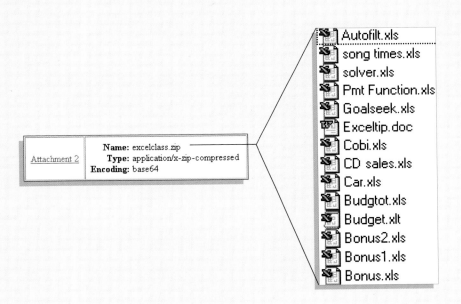

4 As soon as WinZip starts, it automatically decompresses the ZIP file and lists all its component files in the WinZip window. You now have to tell WinZip which files you want to extract and where you want to put them. If you want to extract all the files, start by clicking on the Extract button to display the Extract dialog box.

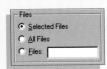

6 To extract only certain files, select them in the WinZip window before clicking on the Extract button (see step 4). If you do this, the Selected Files option button in the Extract dialog box becomes active. Click on it to extract only the selected files. To extract files to more than one folder, just repeat this process, choosing a different folder in the Folders/Drives box each time.

5 The All Files option button is selected by default. This option tells WinZip to extract all the files in the ZIP file. To do so, just choose a folder in the Folders/Drives box to hold the extracted files, and click on the Extract button. If you want to extract files to more than one folder, or if you want to extract only some of the files in the ZIP file, continue with steps 6 and 7. Otherwise, skip to step 8.

How to Attach a URL to an E-Mail Message

Attaching a URL to an e-mail message is a great way to tell a friend about a Web page because it saves you the step of writing down the URL. When you attach a URL, Netscape actually sends a copy of the HTML source code for the Web page to the recipient, so the recipient can view the page with all its formatting intact, and all its links active.

1 Display the Message Composition window; fill in the Mail To, Cc (optional), and Subject text boxes; and type a message if you like. Then click on the Attachment button (or click on the Attach toolbar button) to display the Attachments dialog box.

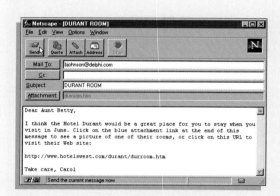

8 Fill in the Mail To and Cc (optional) text boxes, type a message (you can type above and below the link), and click on the Send button.

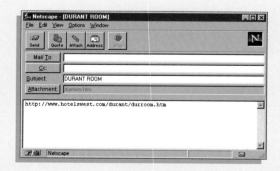

7 Netscape displays the Message Composition window. It uses the title of the Web page as the subject line, it attaches the URL to the message (listing the URL in the Attachment box), and it inserts a hypertext link to the page in the body of the message.

TIP SHEET

▶ **If you just want to include a hypertext link to a Web page in an e-mail message, but don't want to send the Web page as an attachment, type the URL directly into the e-mail message. It will be displayed as a hypertext link when the recipient receives the message.**

▶ **Rather than typing the URL into your e-mail message, you can have Netscape enter it for you. Right-click on a link to the URL in a Web page, choose Copy Link Location from the context menu, click in the e-mail message, and choose Edit, Paste (or press Ctrl+V).**

2 In the Attachments dialog box, click on the Attach Location (URL) button.

3 Netscape displays a dialog box entitled Please Specify a Location to Attach. Type the URL for the Web page in the text box and click on OK. If you don't include the name of an actual page (as in this example), Netscape attaches the default Web page at the Web site you specify.

4 Netscape lists the URL in the Attachments dialog box. Repeat steps 2 and 3 if you want to attach more URLs. Then click on OK.

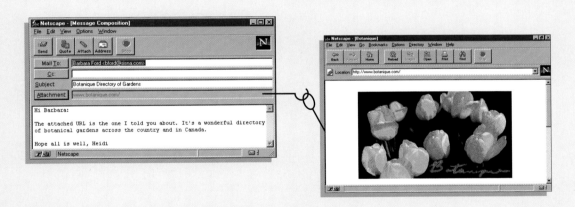

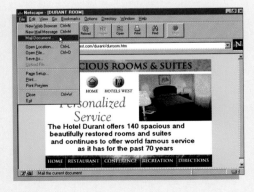

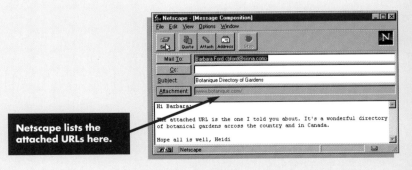

Netscape lists the attached URLs here.

6 If you visit a Web page you want to send to someone, you can send it right from the page by choosing File, Mail Document.

5 In a moment, Netscape displays the URL in the Attachment box in the Message Composition window. Click on the Send button.

How to View an Attached URL

You have to save most attached documents before you can open them because Netscape can't display most document types. However, it can display all Web pages (this is, after all, Netscape's strong suit), so it always displays attached URLs directly in the Message pane. In addition to attached URLs, which actually send a copy of the Web page with the message, messages you receive might contain *hypertext links* to URLs. These links behave differently than attached URLs; they actually take you to the Web page, wherever it lives on the Web, instead of sending a copy of the page along with the message.

▶ ❶ In the Netscape Mail window, click on the message in the Message Header pane.

❻ If you display a message with an attached URL when View, Attachments Inline is selected, the Web page is automatically displayed inline. Here is the same page displayed with View, Attachments Inline turned on. Notice that Netscape can't always display all the formatting when you view a page inline. In this case, it can't display the background color.

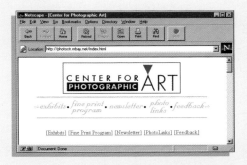

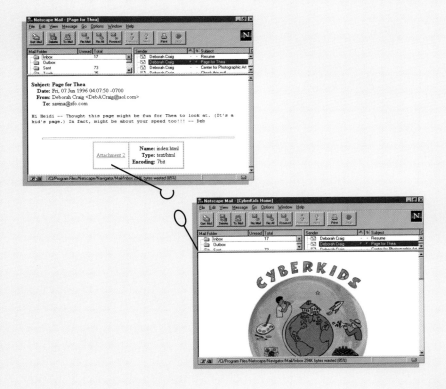

2 If the sender typed the URL into the e-mail message or used the File, Mail Document command, you will see a hypertext link to the Web page. Click on the link to jump to the page.

3 Notice that when you click on a hypertext link in an e-mail message, Netscape automatically switches from the Netscape Mail window to the main Netscape window to display the page.

4 The message might just contain an attached URL and not a hypertext link. If you have View, Attachments As Links selected, you'll see a link like the one shown here. Click on the link to display the page.

5 Netscape temporarily fills up the entire Message pane with the attached Web page, obscuring the rest of the message. (In this example, the Message pane was resized to show you more of the page.) Notice that all the formatting is preserved, including the background color of the page. To bring the rest of the message back into view, click on a different message, and then click back on the message with the attachment.

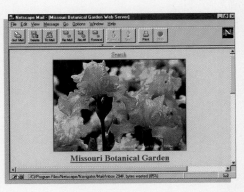

CHAPTER 10

Participating in Newsgroups

 For many years, people have been exchanging ideas, advice, and information in online discussion groups called *news-groups*. Newsgroups are part of an Internet facility called Usenet, and they are distributed by machines called *news servers*.

There are thousands of newsgroups, each focusing on a particular topic. Newsgroups are organized into hierarchies to make them easier to find. Some of the major hierarchies are comp (computers), sci (science), rec (recreation), soc (social issues), and news (newsgroup-related topics). Each hierarchy is divided into branches and possibly subbranches. A newsgroup's name indicates where it fits in a particular hierarchy. For example, the rec.animals.wildlife newsgroup is in the animals branch of the rec hierarchy.

The program you use to access newsgroups is called a *newsreader*. The newsreader used in this chapter is Netscape News, which is integrated into Netscape Navigator. You can also check out other shareware newsreaders such as Free Agent (available at http://www.tucows.com).

Before you experiment with newsgroups, make sure you have told Netscape the name of your ISP's news server. (Choose Options, Mail and News Preferences, click on the Servers tab, and type the name in the News (NNTP) Server text box.)

In this chapter, you learn how to select which newsgroups you want to list in Netscape News, how to read messages, and how to post, reply to, and forward messages. You also get a crash course in newsgroup etiquette, and you learn how to use a service called Deja News that searches across newsgroups for messages on topics you specify.

How to Subscribe and Unsubscribe to a Newsgroup

There are so many newsgroups that individual ISPs can't possibly offer access to them all, so ISPs selectively choose which newsgroups to carry. Even so, the list of newsgroups is likely to be quite long. You can shorten the list by *subscribing* to particular newsgroups. Subscribing is simply the way that you tell your newsreader which newsgroups you want the newsreader to list. (You can always tell the newsreader to show you all the newsgroups carried by your ISP, including the unsubscribed ones, if you choose.) You can subscribe or unsubscribe to any newsgroup at any time.

TIP SHEET

▶ **To unsubscribe to a newsgroup, just clear its check box.**

▶ **The Options, Show New Newsgroups command shows only newsgroups that are new since you last connected to your news server.**

▶ **You can resize the three panes in the Netscape News window by dragging their gray borders.**

▶ **Just above many folders is a newsgroup of the same name. For example, in step 5 there is a newsgroup named rec just above the rec folder. This happens because most hierarchies start out as a single newsgroup. When the postings become too numerous, the participants decide to split the newsgroup into several smaller newsgroups. The original newsgroup is not always removed, however, even though most people start posting messages to the new more specialized newsgroups in the hierarchy.**

▶ **1** Choose Window, Netscape News to display the Netscape News window (shown in the middle of this page). The Newsgroup pane lists the newsgroups carried by your ISP, the Message Header pane lists messages within the selected newsgroup, and the Message Pane displays the contents of the selected message.

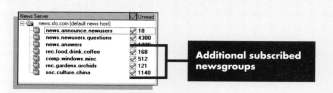

Additional subscribed newsgroups

8 In the example shown here, the user subscribed to four additional newsgroups.

7 After you've subscribed to all the newsgroups that interest you at the moment, choose Options, Show Subscribed Newsgroups to hide all newsgroups but the ones you've subscribed to, or choose Options, Show Active Newsgroups to see only subscribed newsgroups that contain new messages. Choosing one of these two commands will make it easier to navigate in the Netscape News window because you'll have fewer newsgroups to wade through.

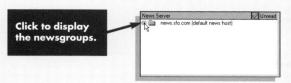

Click to display the newsgroups.

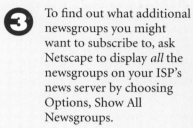

You are subscribed to these three newsgroups automatically.

2 Netscape automatically subscribes you to three newsgroups that contain helpful information and advice for new users. You can tell you're subscribed because of the check marks next to the newsgroup names. If you don't see any newsgroups, click on the plus sign next to the default news host to expand the display. (The *default news host* is your ISP's news server.)

3 To find out what additional newsgroups you might want to subscribe to, ask Netscape to display *all* the newsgroups on your ISP's news server by choosing Options, Show All Newsgroups.

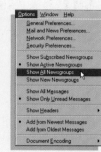

Newsgroup pane

Message Header pane

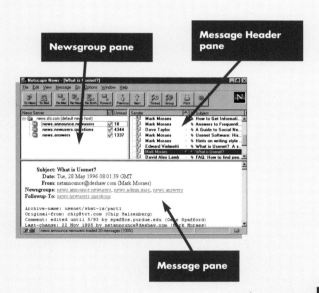

Message pane

This is a hierarchy.

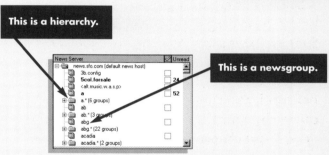

This is a newsgroup.

4 All the newsgroup hierarchies eventually appear in the Newsgroup pane. (This can take several minutes.) The yellow folder icons represent newsgroup hierarchies (or branches within hierarchies). The page icons represent actual newsgroups.

The rec hierarchy contains 564 newsgroups.

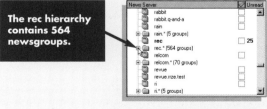

5 As you scroll through the list, you'll see folders for all the main hierarchies (comp, news, rec, and so on), as well as for many others. Netscape lists the number of newsgroups in each hierarchy to the right of the hierarchy name. Click on the plus sign to the left of a hierarchy to expand it, displaying all the newsgroups and branches that hierarchy contains (and then click on the minus sign to collapse the view).

6 Each hierarchy contains some combination of newsgroups and folders (representing branches within the main hierarchy). Continue clicking on the folders until you find a newsgroup that catches your fancy. To subscribe, mark its check box. (Before deciding whether to subscribe to a newsgroup, you'll probably want to read a few of its messages, as discussed on the next page.)

How to Read Newsgroup Messages

R eading newsgroup messages is very similar to reading e-mail. One difference is that Netscape doesn't automatically save newsgroup messages on your computer. Instead, it just lets you view the messages in the newsgroups stored on your ISP's news server. Each time you click on a message to read it, Netscape transfers the information from the server to your computer, so newsgroup messages take longer to display.

TIP SHEET

▶ **If you want to save a message to disk, select the message; choose File, Save As; type a name for the file in the File Name box; and click on the Save button. Netscape saves the message as a plain-text file, which you can then open in any word processing program. It's a good idea to save messages that you're really interested in, because old messages are deleted from newsgroups at regular intervals.**

▶ **To print a message, select the message, click on the Print toolbar button, and then click on OK.**

▶ **The quality of discussion in newsgroups ranges from highly informative to absolutely worthless. Many newsgroups are cluttered with $$$GET RICH QUICK$$$ messages and equally meaningless or tasteless garbage. In Internet parlance, you have to evaluate the "signal-to-noise ratio" of each newsgroup, and if there is more noise than signal, you may want to unsubscribe (or never subscribe in the first place).**

▶ **Newsgroup messages can contain attached documents or URLs. Because you handle attachments to newsgroup messages the same way you handle e-mail attachments, you can refer to Chapter 9 for help.**

▶**1** Choose Window, Netscape News to display the Netscape News window, and then click on the desired newsgroup. You'll see the messages in that group in the Message Header pane. Notice that Netscape automatically *threads* newsgroup messages, organizing all the replies to one message together in one branch. This makes it easier to follow the various discussions. (If this feature is off, you can turn it back on by choosing View, Sort, Thread Messages.)

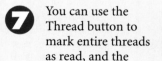
You can mark messages of interest.

8 You can click in the column to the right of the author name in the Message Header pane to place red flags on messages you want to return to later. Once you flag messages, you can use the First Flagged, Next Flagged, and Previous Flagged commands in the Go menu to jump quickly between them.

7 You can use the Thread button to mark entire threads as read, and the Group button to mark entire newsgroups as read. Assuming the Options, Show Only Unread Messages command is turned on, it's helpful to mark threads you're not interested in as read, so that the newsreader won't display them in the future. The same is true with groups if you have the Show Active Newsgroups command turned on.

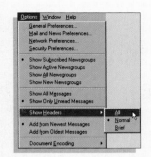

2 Netscape boldfaces new messages and marks them with the green Unread flag. To read a message, simply click on it. Netscape clears the Unread flag and displays the contents of the message in the Message pane. The message begins with the subject and the date, and then lists information about the author and the newsgroups to which the author posted the message. The References line contains links to any previous messages in the current thread.

3 Some newsgroups are *moderated*, meaning that all incoming messages are reviewed to determine whether they are inappropriate, offensive, or unrelated to the newsgroup. The quality of the discussion in moderated groups is often better than that of unmoderated groups. To find out if a newsgroup is moderated, first choose Options, Show Headers, All to show more detailed information at the beginning of each message.

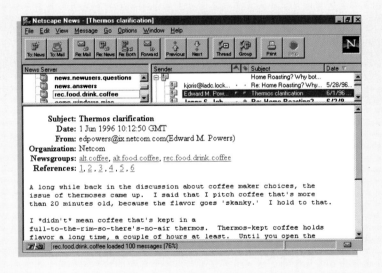

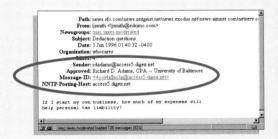

4 Moderated newsgroups have a line called Approved at the beginning of each message, listing the names of the people who moderate the group. (To hide this detailed information, choose Options, Show Header, Normal.)

5 You can change the order in which Netscape lists newsgroup messages by choosing among the four options at the bottom of the View, Sort submenu. The default sort option is By Date, which tells Netscape to list the most recent messages at the top. By Subject and By Author arrange messages alphabetically by subject or author, and By Message Number sorts messages by the order of arrival at the news server.

6 To quickly jump to the next or previous new message, click on the Next and Previous buttons in the toolbar.

How to Post a Newsgroup Message

Here and on the next page, you learn how to jump into a newsgroup discussion and contribute your own two cents. The steps on this page explain how to post a new message; on the next page, you learn how to reply to and forward existing messages. Before you start contributing to a newsgroup, it's a good idea to read "How to Interact in Newsgroups" later in the chapter to learn basic newsgroup etiquette.

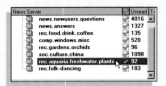

▶ **1** Choose Window, Netscape News, and click on the newsgroup to which you want to post a message.

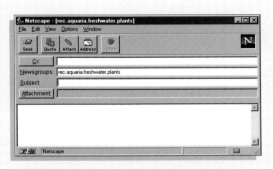

2 Click on the To:News toolbar button (or choose File, New News Message).

3 Netscape displays the Message Composition window. The newsgroup name appears in the title bar and in the Newsgroups text box. If you want to post your message to additional newsgroups, you can add their names to the Newsgroups text box, separating them with commas.

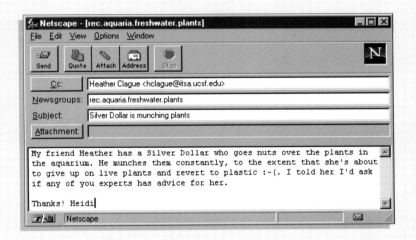

4 If you want to send the message to someone as an e-mail message as well, you can enter the e-mail address in the Cc text box.

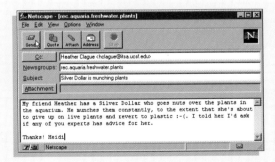

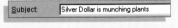

5 Enter a subject for the message in the Subject text box.

6 Type the message, and then click on the Send button. In a moment, you will see the message added to the Message Header pane (unless the group is moderated, in which case the message will be mailed to the moderator for approval before posting).

How to Reply to or Forward a Message

Posting a new message in a newsgroup starts a new thread. In contrast, replying to a message adds your message to an existing thread. As you'll see, there are three ways to reply to a message. And in addition to replying to messages, you can forward them to other people.

▶ **1** Click on the message to which you want to reply.

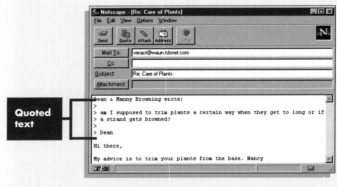

Quoted text

8 As when you're replying to e-mail messages, you may want to quote the portions of newsgroup messages to which you're responding. To do this, click on the Quote button in the Mail Composition window. Netscape inserts the original text in the message, beginning each line with a > symbol. You can type in between the lines of original text and delete any sections you don't need.

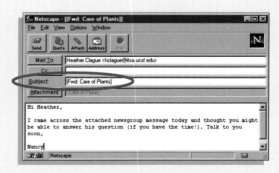

7 The Mail Composition window opens with the subject of the message in the Subject text box (preceded by Fwd: and enclosed within brackets). Enter the e-mail address of the person to whom you're forwarding the message in the Mail To text box. Optionally type a brief message, and click on the Send button.

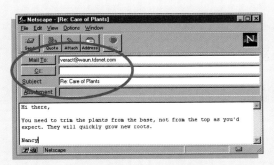

2 Next, click on one of three buttons in the toolbar: Re:Mail, Re:News, or Re:Both. Once you've clicked on one of the buttons, type your response, and click on the Send button.

3 The Re:Mail button lets you send an e-mail reply to the author without sending a message to the newsgroup. Clicking on this button opens the Message Composition window with the author's e-mail address in the Mail To text box and the subject from the original e-mail message in the Subject text box (preceded by Re:).

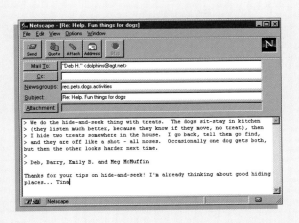

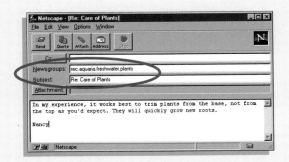

4 The Re:News button posts a reply to the newsgroup, but does not send an e-mail reply to the author. Clicking on this button opens the Message Composition window with the name of the newsgroup in the Newsgroups text box and the subject from the original e-mail message in the Subject text box (preceded by Re:).

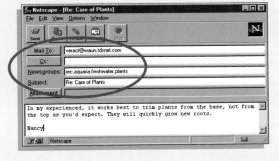

6 To forward a newsgroup message to another person, select the message, and then click on the toolbar Forward button.

5 As you might guess, the Re:Both button lets you send an e-mail reply to the author and a message to the newsgroup. Clicking on this button opens the Message Composition window with the author's e-mail address in the Mail To text box, the newsgroup name in the Newsgroups text box, and the subject of the original message in the Subject text box (preceded by Re:).

How to Interact in Newsgroups

If you are intrigued with the idea of partici-pating in a newsgroup but aren't sure what the ground rules are, the suggestions on this page should help you feel comfortable jumping into a discussion. A word of warning: Newsgroups are a forum for everyone. As in the real (noncyber world), you'll meet some people who are polite and responsible, and others who are rude and thoughtless. If the tone of a newsgroup is unfriendly, it might not be worth participating in the discussion even if the topic is of interest to you.

 1 When you find a newsgroup you'd like to participate in, read other people's mes-sages for a while before posting your own. This way, you can avoid posting questions that have already been asked many times by other people, and you can get a feel for the culture of the particular group.

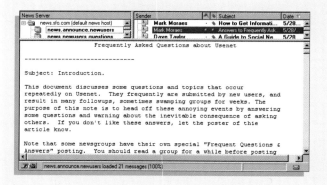

 Read FAQs whenever you find them. FAQs (*Frequently Asked Questions*) are lists of answers to common questions. Many newsgroups regu-larly post FAQs for newcomers, and newsgroups ending with .answers contain only FAQs. The three newsgroups that Netscape automatically subscribes you to (news.announce.newusers, news.newusers.questions, and news.answers) contain FAQs on everything you need to know about participating in newsgroups.

2 If you see a large number of messages you don't like, it's better simply to un-subscribe from the group than to write numerous messages criticizing what you see. That tactic only winds up filling the newsgroup with attacks and counterat-tacks, the group loses its original focus, and no one benefits.

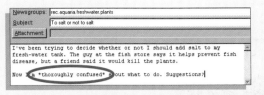

3 It is not a good idea to use all uppercase in newsgroup mail messages because it seems as though you're SHOUTING, and you'll come across as boorish even if that wasn't your intention. (If you write a lot of e-mail, you probably already know this.) A better way to emphasize text is to surround it with *asterisks*.

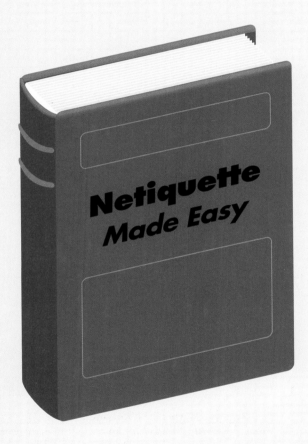

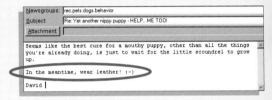

4 If you want to add a bit of humor or sarcasm to a message, you can use a smiley to make sure people under-stand that you're joking. A *smiley* is a sequence of characters that, when viewed sideways, looks like a facial expression. Some examples are :-) to express a smile, ;-) to show a wink, and :-(to express sadness.

5 Keep your messages brief and to the point, and use meaningful subject lines. (The subject "How do I treat my fish for ich?" is more meaningful than "Help!") If you're asking for help, supply enough informa-tion about your situation that people can to give you the assistance you need.

6 Be careful not to post messages in newsgroups where they don't really belong. Newsgroups deteri-orate in quality when they contain lots of irrelevant messages, and such postings are likely to anger other readers. Along the same lines, avoid posting messages to sell a service or product unless the newsgroup was designed for commercial messages.

How to Search Newsgroups with Deja News

One of the trickier aspects of working with newsgroups is finding messages that discuss a particular topic. One company on the Web that addresses this problem is Deja News. Deja News provides a fast and easy-to-use service that searches across all newsgroups for messages matching the criteria you specify. At present, Deja News doesn't charge you to use its service.

 1 In the main Netscape Navigator window, type the URL **http://dejanews.com** in the Location text box and press Enter to jump to the Deja News Web site.

▶ To learn about searching for other resources on the Internet, refer to Chapter 16.

▶ The Power Search! Button lets you specify whether Deja News should look for newsgroups messages that contain *all* the words you enter as your Search Criteria, or *any* of the words. It also lets you limit your search by newsgroup, date, or author.

▶ If a message you posted to a newsgroup turns up in someone's search results, he or she can display your author profile (see step 6) to see a list of *all* the newsgroups to which you've recently posted messages. People who participate in a wide variety of newsgroups might want to keep in mind that this information is a matter of public record.

 If you want to perform a more specialized search, click on the Power Search! button at the top of Deja News' home page. To get help on using Deja News, click on the Help Index button.

2 Enter your search criteria (also called a *query*) in the Quick Search For text box. In this example, Deja News will search for all newsgroup messages that contain the word *pickles*.

3 After a moment, Deja News displays the results of the search (also called a *hitlist*) with the messages that most closely match your criteria listed at top. For each message, Deja News lists the date, the subject line, the newsgroup containing the message, and the name of the author. To read a message, click on the subject.

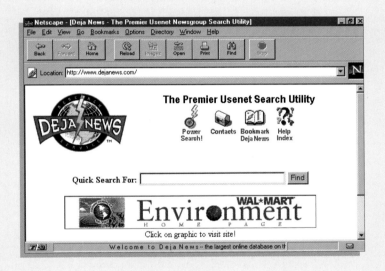

4 Deja News displays the message. (In this example, only the message header information is visible without scrolling.) You can use the buttons at the top of the window to read other messages in the hitlist, to post a message to the newsgroup, to send e-mail to the author, and so on.

6 Deja News displays an author profile, which includes a list of all the newsgroups to which the author has posted messages in the last month.

5 If you want to find out more about the author of a message, click on his or her name in the search results.

CHAPTER 11

Electronic Mailing Lists

 Like newsgroups, mailing lists give people a forum for sharing thoughts, views, and advice about a particular topic. But unlike most newsgroups, many mailing lists are *moderated*, meaning that someone screens the contributions to make sure that their content and tone are appropriate for the list.

Stated simply, a *mailing list* (also called an *e-mail discussion group*) is a list of e-mail addresses. You join (*subscribe* to) a mailing list by asking the person in charge, called the *list administrator* or *list owner*, to add your address to the list. Once you've joined, you receive copies of all the e-mail sent to the list. By the same token, when you send your own message to the list, it gets sent to all the other subscribers.

Although many mailing lists function as discussion groups, others are used primarily as a means of distributing information. A volunteer organization might use a mailing list to send out its monthly newsletter, for example. Mailing lists can also be either public or private. Public lists are open to anyone who wants to join, while private lists usually have requirements for participation. For example, the K9 Police mailing list is only open to police who handle police dogs. Some list administrators also put a cap on the number of subscribers to keep the volume of mail at a manageable level.

In this chapter, you learn how to join and withdraw from a mailing list, how to contribute messages to a mailing list, and how to read incoming messages. Finally, you get some suggestions for finding mailing lists of interest. Because mailing lists are based on e-mail, you need to be familiar with the information in Chapter 8 before diving into this chapter.

How to Join a Mailing List

Most mailing lists use software programs to process subscription requests automatically. The most widely used program is LISTSERV, so the examples on this page show commands for working with LISTSERV lists. Two other commonly used list-management programs are Majordomo and Listproc. Although the techniques for subscribing and unsubscribing are basically the same for all automated lists, the syntax of the commands varies depending on which program is handling the requests, so make sure to read the instructions for each list carefully. (Whether you find out about a list through word of mouth, on a Web site, or in a book, you will usually get some instructions for subscribing.)

TIP SHEET

▶ **It's a great idea to create a separate mail folder for each mailing list you join, and save the confirmation and welcome messages in these folders. This will make it easy to refer to the messages when you need a reminder of how to issue a command—for example, how to issue the command to stop receiving mail from the list when you're on vacation.**

▶ **Be careful about joining too many mailing lists! Your inbox could be literally flooded with hundreds of messages a day.**

▶ **Many lists allow you to reduce the sheer number of e-mail messages by sending a command to the administrative address requesting that messages get sent to you in *digest* form. This option tells the list-management software to consolidate the messages into batches instead of sending them to you individually.**

▶ **If you enjoy a mailing list you've subscribed to, consider sending a thank you note to the list owner. Running a mailing list takes a lot of work!**

 1 Every mailing list has two e-mail addresses with completely different purposes:
  ▶ *List address:* Use this address to contribute to the actual discussion; mail you send to the list address is distributed to all the subscribers.
  ▶ *Administrative address:* Use this address to subscribe, unsubscribe, get help, or customize the way the list works. Messages you send to this address are usually handled automatically. Be *very careful* not to send administrative messages to the list address! If you do, you'll end up sending them to all the subscribers—a surefire way to annoy a lot of people.

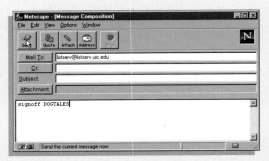

8 To unsubscribe from a mailing list, send a message to the *administrative address.* Leave the subject line blank, and type the command **signoff *listname*** in the subject area. You'll receive a brief message stating that your request was received, and within the next day or so, you'll receive confirmation that you've been removed from the list.

 7 The LISTSERV software sends you a confirmation when you've been added to the list. (If the list is public, you'll get a confirmation in a day or two.) You should save this message in a mail folder because it gives you the list address, tells you how to unsubscribe, and explains how to customize the way the list works. (You might also receive a welcome message from the list administrator telling you more about the "culture" of the list, and describing guidelines for maintaining a positive atmosphere in the discussion.)

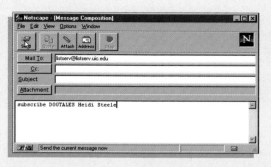

Use the administrative address to subscribe to the list.

2 To subscribe to a list, first display Netscape Mail's Message Composition window, and then type the *administrative address* in the Mail To text box. Leave the Subject text box blank (unless instructed to do otherwise).

3 Type the command to subscribe to the list in the text area. Most LISTSERV mailing lists use this syntax: subscribe *listname yourfirstname yourlastname*. In this example, I typed the command **subscribe DOGTALES Heidi Steele** to subscribe to a mailing list about animal-assisted therapy called *dogtales*. (Mailing-list names are often displayed in uppercase, but the commands are not actually case sensitive.) Send the subscription request, and click on OK when Netscape asks if you want to send a message with no subject.

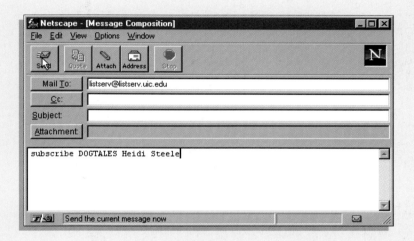

4 Soon you should receive an automated message asking that you confirm your identity by replying to the message with the word *OK*.

6 If the list is private, the list administrator will probably request further information about you. The message will likely include questions about your occupation, your reasons for wanting to join the list, and so on. In your reply, quote the original message where appropriate so that it's clear which questions you're answering. Within a week or two, you'll (hopefully!) receive a confirmation such as the one shown in step 7.

5 Next, a message informs you that your request has been forwarded to the list owner. You haven't been added to the list yet; this message just lets you know that your request is being processed.

How to Participate in a Mailing List

Assuming you already know how to send and receive e-mail, you will have no difficulty participating in mailing lists. E-mail from mailing lists arrives in your inbox just like your other mail. The subject lines will help you distinguish which messages come from mailing lists, and after a while, you'll start to recognize the names of frequent contributors.

> **Use the list address to send mail to the list.**

Mail To:	dogtales@listserv.uic.edu
Cc:	
Subject:	Working with Children

1 To send a message to all the subscribers to a list, display the Message Composition window, type the *list address* in the Mail To text box, and type a descriptive subject in the Subject text box.

7 You can forward, delete, save, and print mailing-list messages as you would other e-mail messages. If you need help with these tasks, refer to Chapter 8.

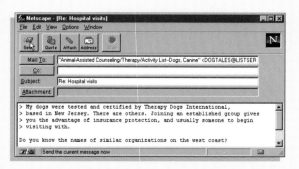

6 Type your message, quoting only as much of the original text as needed to provide a context for what you have to say. Then send the message.

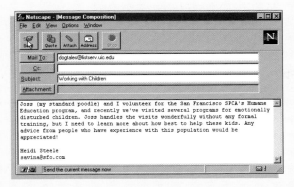

2 Compose and send your message. Remember that many people will read the message, so it's worth taking a moment to make sure it's coherent, reasonably free of typos, and polite. By default, LISTSERV doesn't send you copies of your own contributions to a list, although your confirmation message should explain how to change this setting. After you send your message, you will likely get a confirmation that your message has been distributed to the members of the list.

3 You can reply to a mailing-list message as you would reply to any other e-mail message, by clicking on it and clicking on the Re:Mail toolbar button.

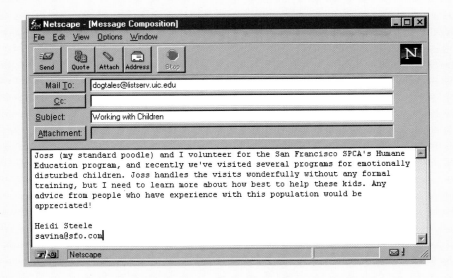

4 Most mail programs, including Netscape Mail, assume you want to reply to the list address so that your message gets sent to all the subscribers.

5 If you instead want to send a private reply to the sender only, replace the list address in the Mail To text box with the sender's e-mail address. It's good to do this when your message is very brief—as in "I agree" or "Me too"—and isn't important enough to send to all the other subscribers. Some list owners encourage people to conduct most discussions in private e-mail, and they reserve the mailing list for bulletins and announcements.

How to Find Out about Mailing Lists

There is no single strategy for finding out about all mailing lists. Private mailing lists are by definition not deliberately publicized; in fact, the best way to find out about them is through word of mouth. On the other hand, public mailing lists are much easier to locate, especially if you use one of the many "lists of lists" on the Internet. This page describes how to use two of the most popular mailing-list databases.

TIP SHEET

▶ **One other way to find publicly available mailing lists is to search on the words *mailing list* in a search service such as Yahoo! You'll learn how to use search services in Chapter 16.**

▶ **The Liszt service makes it easy to subscribe to a mailing list you've found in their database. First read the information on how to subscribe, and then click on the link for the administrative address. Liszt displays the Message Composition window with the administrative address already entered in the Mail To text box. Type the subscription command and click on the Send button.**

▶ **If you want to start your own mailing list, a good place to begin gathering information is http://www.lsoft.com, the Web site of L-Soft International. This company distributes the LISTSERV software, which now includes a version for Windows 95.**

 1 The most extensive list of mailing lists is the Liszt service at http://www.liszt.com (shown in the middle of the page). Liszt continuously searches the Internet for new mailing lists and adds them to the database. To respect privacy, it doesn't include any mailing list whose name or description contains the word *private*.

Potbellied Pigs

Contact: pbplserv@candlelight.com

Purpose: To discuss and share information regarding potbellied pigs such as feeding, medical, maintainence, and other potbellied pig (PBP) specific topic. Listserver open to owners, breeders, and those wishing information.

To subscribe, send email to
    pbplserv@candlelight.com
and on the Subject: line, put
    SUBSCRIBE

9 You see a list of all the mailing lists that relate to that particular topic. Clicking on an individual list gives you a description and contact information about the list.

8 Click on a subject of interest.

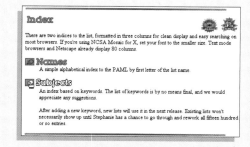

7 Click on Subjects to search for mailing lists by topic.

2 To search for a mailing list using Liszt, start by typing a word or phrase to describe the type of mailing list you're looking for, and then press Enter or click on the Search button. (If Netscape displays its standard security warning about submitting information to a Web site, click on Continue.)

3 After a moment, Liszt displays all the mailing lists whose names or descriptions contain the search text. Click on a list to get more detailed information about how to subscribe to it. Some lists include the [info] icon. Clicking on this icon displays a description of the purpose of the list.

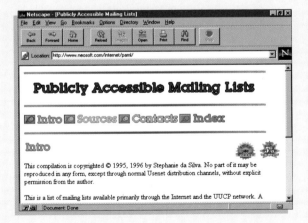

4 Liszt gives you the list and administrative addresses for the list as well as thorough instructions on how to subscribe. Note that Liszt plasters its Web pages with reminders *not* to send subscription-type requests to the list address.

5 Publicly Accessible Mailing Lists (shown in the middle of the page) is another well-known list of mailing lists. To reach it, enter the URL **http://www.neosoft.com/internet/paml**. As its name implies, this list includes only public mailing lists, and it provides thorough information on each list.

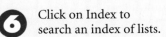

6 Click on Index to search an index of lists.

CHAPTER 12

Transferring Files with FTP

Back when the Web was still a gleam in a programmer's eye, people were already downloading files from Internet computers (and uploading them as well) using a protocol called FTP (File Transfer Protocol). Now that the Web has become so popular, many companies make files available for downloading at their Web sites. However, individuals and companies have continued to use FTP because it is often the most convenient and flexible way to transfer files between computers on the Internet. FTP lets you easily send binary files, and even computers that don't have Web server or browser support can usually handle FTP. (Remember that when you send binary files as e-mail attachments, Netscape has to first encode them as plain-text files, and the program at the receiving end has to decode them.)

FTP uses FTP-client software built into your browser to retrieve or send files between your computer and host computers running FTP-server software. (These computers are commonly called *FTP sites.*) In addition to downloading files—including programs, graphics, text documents, and so on—from FTP sites around the world, you can upload files to FTP sites. There are plenty of situations in which this comes in handy. For example, if you maintain your own Web site at your ISP, FTP is the easiest way to copy the Web pages you create on your own computer onto your ISP's computer (see Chapter 21).

Netscape and other browsers don't handle FTP as flexibly as some stand-alone FTP programs do, so if you use FTP frequently, you might want to get a shareware FTP program such as CuteFTP or WS_FTP (both available through http://www.tucows.com).

In this chapter, you learn a few ways to connect to and navigate in an FTP site, and then you learn how to download and upload files.

How to Connect to an FTP Site

To connect to an FTP site, you need to know the name of an account on the FTP server. In other words, you need to log in with a user name and password so that the server knows who you are. Publicly accessible FTP sites expect you to use a special account called *anonymous.* Unless you tell Netscape otherwise, it assumes that you want to connect to FTP sites as an anonymous user, and it supplies the server with the user name *anonymous* and a password consisting of your own e-mail address. If you have a personal account on a host computer (your ISP, for example), you'll probably want to log onto the computer's FTP server using this account, because it will give you access to files that are not available to anonymous users.

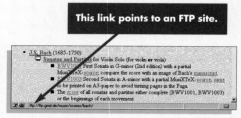

This link points to an FTP site.

1 One way to connect to an FTP site as an anonymous user is to click on a link to an FTP site in a Web page. You can tell if a link points to an FTP site because the URL displayed in the status bar begins with *ftp://.* (All URLs for FTP sites begin this way.) In this example, the URL for the J.S. Bach link points to the music/scores/bach directory at an FTP site in Germany called ftp.gmd.de.

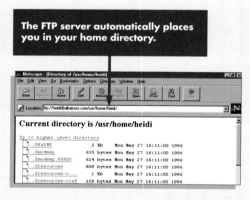

The FTP server automatically places you in your home directory.

7 Netscape displays the FTP site, and the server places you in your home directory, to which you probably have rights.

6 When you log into an FTP site using a personal account, the host computer prompts you for a password. Type it in and click on OK. (Sending your password this way can be a security risk. Some stand-alone FTP programs avoid sending your password and use other more secure ways to verify who you are to the server.)

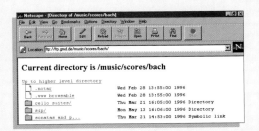

2 Clicking on the link displays the FTP site. (You'll find out how to navigate in an FTP site on the next page.)

3 If you know (or can guess) the URL for an FTP site, you can connect to it as an anonymous user without a link on a Web page. Just type the URL for the site into the Location text box and press Enter. In this example, the user is connecting to the FTP site of an ISP called San Francisco Online.

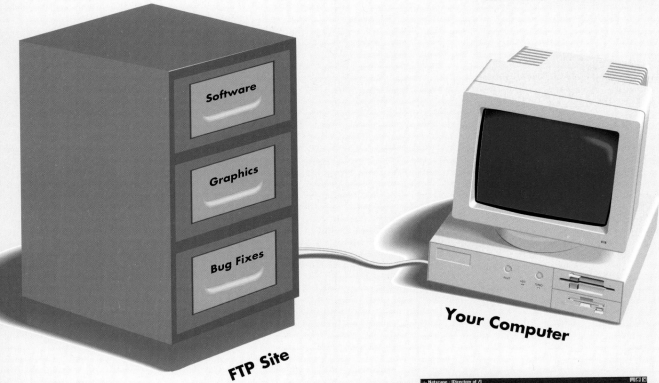

Your Computer

FTP Site

5 To log into an FTP server using a personal account, you need to insert your user name in the URL just after the ftp://. In this example, I typed the URL **ftp://heidi@albatross.com** to log into a computer named *albatross.com* with a user name of *heidi*. (To log into the same computer as an anonymous user, I'd type the URL **ftp://albatross.com**).

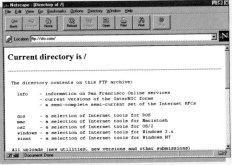

4 Netscape connects to the requested FTP site, and the FTP server places you in the top-level directory of the area on the host computer to which anonymous users have rights.

How to Navigate in an FTP Site

The directory structure at FTP sites is similar to the organization of folders on your hard disk. In many cases, anonymous users can download files stored in a directory called /pub and its subdirectories, and can upload files to a directory called /incoming. If you log into an FTP server with a personal account, you'll usually be given access to a personal directory—called your *home* directory—and its subdirectories.

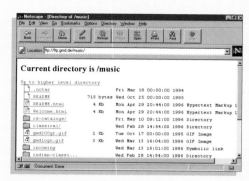

▶ **①** The current directory is always displayed at the top of the screen with forward slashes (/) separating the levels of the directory structure, and the contents of the directory are listed underneath. Netscape uses various page icons to represent different types of files, and yellow folder icons to represent subdirectories.

TIP SHEET

▶ Sometimes administrators hide files for security reasons, so directories that appear to be empty may in fact contain files.

▶ If you try clicking on a directory to which you haven't been granted access, Netscape displays a message box telling you that it is unable to find that file or directory.

Read the README

```
Up to higher level directory
    .notar                    Fri Mar 18 00:00:00 1994
    README          715 bytes Wed Oct 25 00:00:00 1995
    README.html     4 Kb      Mon Apr 29 20:44:00 1996
    Welcome.html    4 Kb      Mon Apr 29 20:44:00 1996
```

2 When you first connect to a site, click on links for any files called README or Welcome. These files usually tell you what materials are stored at the FTP archive, and what the various directories contain. (In this example, two of the files have the .html extension—these are Web pages. FTP and Web resources frequently overlap, so you can often access Web pages from an FTP server and FTP resources from a Web page. You can read either the HTML or plain text version of the README and Welcome files.)

3 Netscape displays the README file. When you're done reading the README, click on the Back toolbar button.

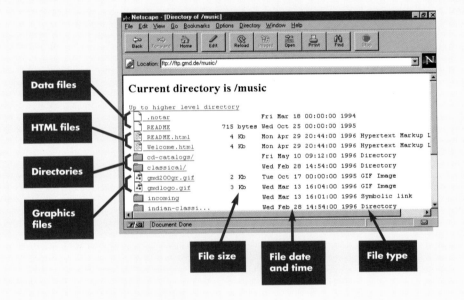

Data files

HTML files

Directories

Graphics files

File size

File date and time

File type

4 To move to a subdirectory, click on its link.

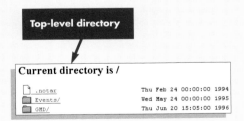

Top-level directory

6 If you continue to click on the Up to Higher Level Directory link, you eventually reach the top-level directory to which you have been granted access. This directory is indicated by a single forward slash (/).

5 Netscape displays the contents of the subdirectory. To move back up to the previous directory, click on the Up to Higher Level Directory link at the top of the list.

How to Download a File from an FTP Site

Before you download a file, read the relevant README files to find out about any operating system, hardware, or software requirements. Also, you need to be careful about avoiding viruses when you download files from FTP sites—as when you download from Web pages. Try to download from well-established, reputable FTP sites, and remember that it's a good idea to check downloaded programs with anti-virus software before installing them. (See Chapter 15 to learn about anti-virus software.)

TIP SHEET

▶ **Many FTP sites contain files that are compressed in the Z or GZ format. (The figure in step 2 includes two GZ files.) WinZip can unzip these files for you.**

▶ **Other shareware FTP programs let you transfer files more efficiently than you can with Netscape. For example, CuteFTP (http://www.cuteftp.com) lets you use drag-and-drop to transfer files between your computer and the FTP server. You can upload or download several files at once, and if you're connecting using a personal account, CuteFTP can remember your user name and password and supply it to the server for you.**

▶ **Netscape assumes you want to do a *binary* file transfer. Binary transfers work to transfer both binary and ASCII files. Some stand-alone FTP programs let you set the transfer type to *binary* or *ASCII*. If you're using one of these programs, be sure to use the binary transfer type if the file is binary; a binary file won't transfer properly if you have the transfer type set to ASCII.**

1 Display the directory that contains the file you want to download.

6 Once you've saved the file on your hard disk, you can open it using the appropriate software. Here is the downloaded file, one of J.S. Bach's handwritten scores, opened in a shareware graphics program called PaintShop Pro.

Current directory is
/music/scores/bach/sonatas_and_partitas

```
Up to higher level directory
   .notar                         Wed Feb 28 13:55:00 1996
   .www browsable                 Wed Feb 28 13:55:00 1996
   book1003.ps.gz      403 Kb     Mon May 13 15:52:00 1996
   bwv1001.gif          99 Kb     Wed Mar 23 00:00:00 1994
   bwv1001.ps.gz       325 Kb     Mon May 13 15:52:00 1996
```

② One method for downloading a file is to save the file to your disk without trying to display it in the browser window. To do this, *Shift+click* on the link for the file, and then skip to step 4. Another method is to try to display the file in the browser window first. To do this, *click* on the link for the file, and then go to the next step. Netscape may or may not be able to display the file properly, because it only recognizes certain file types.

③ Netscape successfully displays the file in this example because it recognizes the GIF file type. Chances are good, however, that the file will *not* be a type that Netscape can display properly, in which case it will either display an empty window or a bunch of garbage characters. If you have displayed the file and want to save it, choose File, Save As. (Even if Netscape doesn't display the file correctly, you can still save it with File, Save As.)

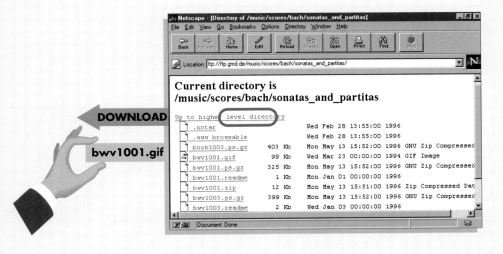

④ In the Save As dialog box, choose a folder for the file in the Save In drop-down list, keep the existing file name, and click on the Save button.

⑤ Netscape displays the Saving Location dialog box as it's saving the file.

How to Upload a File to an FTP Site

Uploading a file to a company FTP server is sometimes the most expedient way of sending a file, especially if it's a binary file. For instance, if the person you're sending to isn't that savvy about receiving binary e-mail attachments or doesn't have the necessary software, it might be easiest for you to FTP the file to the person's company computer. And if you're maintaining a Web site at your ISP, FTP is a convenient way to transfer Web pages from your computer to the Web site.

❶ Connect to an FTP site and move to the directory to which you want to upload file. (If you're using anonymous FTP, you will probably upload the file into the /incoming directory.)

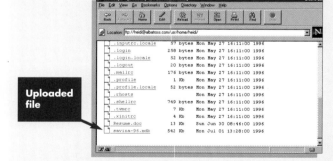

Uploaded file

❼ The file is now listed in the directory on the FTP server.

2 Choose File, Upload File to display the File Upload dialog box.

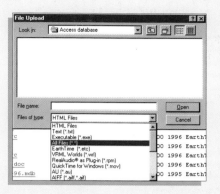

3 Netscape assumes you want to upload a Web page (an HTML document). If you want to upload a different type of file, select the type in the Files of Type drop-down list. If you want to see all the files, choose All Files (*.*).

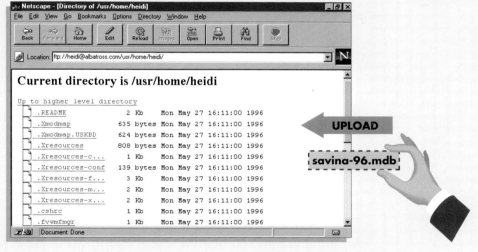

UPLOAD

savina-96.mdb

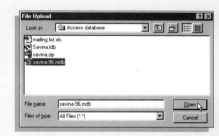

4 Use the Look In drop-down list to display the folder that contains the file, click on the file name, and click on the Open button.

5 Netscape displays a message box telling you that it's uploading the file.

6 As soon as it finishes uploading the file, Netscape displays a message box telling you that the upload was successful. Click on the OK button.

CHAPTER 13

Telnet

 In the pre-Web era, Telnet was a major player among Internet software programs because it was one of the best tools for accessing information on remote computers. Average folk used Telnet to connect to databases at libraries, universities, and scientific institutions around the world, and computer people used it to troubleshoot problems and log into remote computers.

Although computer gurus still use Telnet extensively, most of us have abandoned it in favor of the Web. The remote applications you connect to via Telnet usually have a text-based interface and clunky commands, and many organizations now let you search their online databases through Web sites. Some resources are still only available via Telnet, however, so it's a good idea to learn the basics of working with this tool.

Like FTP, Telnet is a client/server application. Your computer uses a Telnet-client program to connect to a remote computer (usually a UNIX system) running a Telnet-server program. During a Telnet session, your computer functions as a terminal connected to the remote computer: You can type commands at your keyboard to use programs on the remote computer, just as if you were typing on that computer's keyboard.

In this chapter, you learn how to configure Netscape to use a simple Telnet-client program that comes with Windows 95, you learn a few ways of connecting to a Telnet site, and you see an example of how to navigate in a remote application during a Telnet session.

How to Set Up Netscape to Use Telnet

Configuring Netscape to use the Telnet program that comes with Windows 95 is a simple process that you only have to do once. After you've followed the steps on this page, Netscape automatically launches the Telnet program and attempts to connect to the remote computer whenever you tell it to jump to a Telnet site.

▶ **You can configure Netscape to use any Telnet program you like, and there are several good third-party programs available at software archives such as Tucows (http://www.tucows.com). However, the Windows 95 Telnet application probably has all the capabilities you need.**

▶ **You don't have to have Netscape open to use Telnet. Just establish a connection to your ISP, and then start the Telnet application. (If you use Telnet independently of Netscape, you might want to create a shortcut for the program on your desktop.)**

▶ **①** Choose the Options, General Preferences command in Netscape to display the Preferences dialog box.

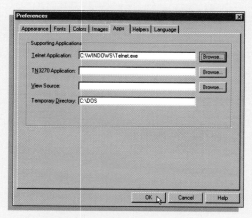

⑤ Now the Apps tab of the Preferences dialog box lists the path and file name of the Telnet application. Click on the OK button to close the dialog box.

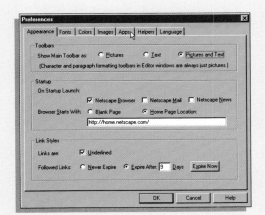

2 Click on the Apps tab at the top of the dialog box.

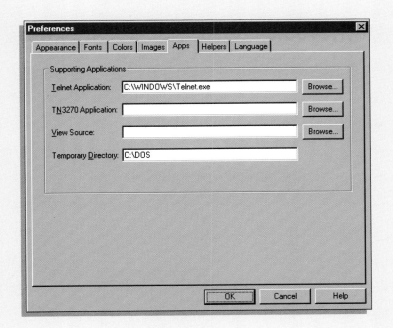

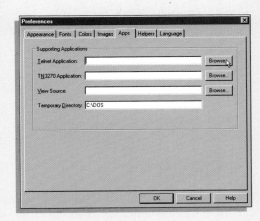

3 Click on the Browse button to the right of the Telnet Application text box to display the Select a Telnet Application dialog box.

4 The Telnet program is stored in your Windows folder. Use the Look In drop-down list to display the contents of the Windows folder, click on the file named Telnet.exe (depending on your Windows 95 configuration, you may not see the .exe extension), and click on the Open button.

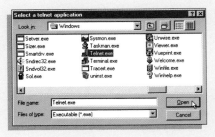

How to Connect to a Telnet Site

You can use any of the methods described on this page to connect to a Telnet site. After you're connected, the Telnet server will ask you for a login name. If you're connecting to a public site, the name will either be listed in whatever resource you used to find out about the site (a book or a Web site, for example) or in the first screen you see when you connect. (Public sites usually don't require passwords.) If, however, you're connecting to a computer on which you have a personal account, you will need to enter your regular user name and password.

TIP SHEET

▸ When you're finished with a Telnet session, you need to log off the remote computer. The commands for logging off vary from site to site, but the most typical command on UNIX systems is logout. (Others are exit, quit, and bye.) If you can't figure out what command to type, you can choose Connect, Disconnect to terminate the connection. You should only use this option as a last resort, however, because it may not properly close your session on the remote computer.

▸ Some Telnet servers require that you connect to a nonstandard port on the remote computer. If this is the case, you will see a colon followed by the port number at the end of the URL. If you're using the Connect dialog box to establish the connection, type the port number in the Port list box.

▸ The Telnet client and server programs have to agree on what type of terminal your computer will emulate. The default type is VT100, which usually works just fine. If you need to change the terminal type, you can choose a different type from the TermType list in the Connect dialog box.

1 One way to connect to a Telnet site is to click on a link to a Telnet URL in a Web page. (All Telnet URLs begin with *telnet://*). The URL shown here points to Book Stacks Unlimited, a bookstore that lets you order books online.

8 Telnet makes the connection, and the remote computer prompts you for a login name.

7 Type a new Telnet site in the Host Name box (omitting the *telnet://* at the beginning of the URL), leave the Port and TermType settings as is, and click on the Connect button. In this example, the remote computer is called albatross.com.

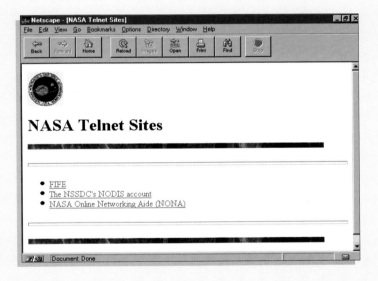

Netscape launches the Telnet program, which starts a Telnet session with the remote computer. Note that because this Telnet site is open to the public, it tells you what to enter as your login name.

Another way to connect to a Telnet site is to type a Telnet URL in Netscape's Location text box and press Enter. Here, the URL points to the Telnet server at San Francisco Online.

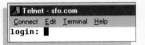

Again, Netscape starts the Telnet application, which then contacts the remote computer. Note that San Francisco Online's computer is not a public Telnet site, so you need to enter the user name and password for an existing account to establish a Telnet session.

After Netscape starts the Telnet program, display the Connect menu. The sites you've visited recently are displayed at the bottom of the menu. If you see the one you want, click on it to create the connection. If the site isn't listed, choose Remote System to display the Connect dialog box.

One other way to connect to a Telnet site is to launch the Telnet program first, and then contact the site. This method is convenient if you're contacting a site you've already visited, because the Telnet program keeps track of sites you've been to before and lets you choose them with a click of the mouse. Begin by typing **telnet:** in the Location text box and pressing Enter.

How to Navigate in a Remote Application

During a Telnet session, you can issue commands to your local Telnet-client program by clicking on menu options. However, there is no consistent set of keyboard commands for navigating in every remote Telnet application (although Telnet applications do have a consistently unattractive interface). The best approach is to read onscreen instructions carefully, and experiment to see what works.

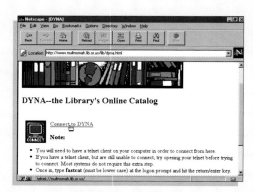

▶ **1** This Web page is part of the Web site for the Multnomah County Library in Portland, Oregon (http://www.multnomah.lib.or.us). Clicking on the Connect to DYNA link takes you to the library's online catalog. When you point to the link, Netscape displays a Telnet URL in the status bar. The Web page reminds you that you need a Telnet client to use the service, indicates what login name to use (*fastcat*), and tells you to type the name in lowercase letters.

8 Type **20** to choose the Logoff command. After the remote computer terminates the connection, the local Telnet application displays the message box shown here. Click on OK to close the message box, and then click on the Close button in the upper-right corner of the Telnet window to close the program.

TIP SHEET

▶ **If you don't see the characters you type on screen during a Telnet session, choose Terminal, Preferences, mark the Local Echo check box, and click on OK. If you see two of each character you type, follow the same steps, but clear the Local Echo check box.**

▶ **If you want to save the contents of a Telnet session to a text file on disk, choose Terminal, Start Logging after you've started the session. In the Open Log File dialog box, choose a name and location for the file, and click on Open. From this point on, all that you see on screen is saved to the file you specified. When you want to stop logging, choose Terminal, Stop Logging.**

7 You're presented with information about the status and location of each copy of *Cold Sassy Tree* in the library system. After reading the information, you can return to the Main Search Menu shown in step 3 by typing **so** and pressing Enter (for the Start Over command).

2 Clicking on the link launches the Telnet application and connects you to the remote computer. Type the login name at the prompt and press Enter.

3 After confirming you want to use VT100 terminal emulation (this is almost always what you want) and quitting the library's news bulletin (by pressing Q and then Enter twice), you're presented with the Main Search Menu. Type the number for the menu option you want and press Enter. Here, I typed **1** to search the catalog by title.

4 The Telnet server prompts you for a title, and I typed **Cold Sassy Tree**, the title of one of my favorite novels.

6 The server shows you detailed information about the book. Here, I pressed Enter to get information about copy status.

5 Next, the server displays the section of the alphabetical list of titles that contains the title you typed. At the prompt, I typed the line number 3 and pressed Enter to get more information about the book.

CHAPTER 14

Gopher

 Gopher is yet another Internet navigation tool that has been eclipsed by the Web. Designed to help people locate resources on the Internet, gopher was for many years one of the most useful Internet tools.

Gopher lets you use a system of text-based menus to track down Internet resources. Individual menu items point to resources (such as other gopher menus, FTP sites, Telnet sites, Web sites, and files) that are stored on the local system or on computers in some other part of the world. And because gopher menus are designed by lots of different people, their organization and content varies considerably from site to site.

Gopher menus are stored on gopher servers, and you view them by using a gopher-client program. Because Netscape includes a built-in gopher client, you can access gopher servers simply by clicking on links in Web pages, or by typing gopher URLs into the Location text box.

If you normally access the Internet through the Web, you won't have much need to deliberately search out gopher servers, since the search services on the Web (described in Chapter 16) are now the easiest means of finding Internet resources. However, you may stumble across gopher sites while you're browsing the Internet, so it's worth taking a quick look at them.

Visiting a Gopher Site

Connecting to and navigating in a gopher site should seem familiar, since it is so much like visiting an FTP site (see Chapter 12).

This URL points to a gopher site.

1 One way to jump to a gopher site is to click on a link in a Web page. This link points to a gopher URL for Amnesty International. As you might be able to guess by now, all gopher URLs begin with *gopher://*.

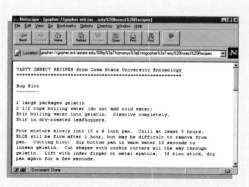

7 Clicking on the link displays the file. Unfortunately for you, only the first of the four recipes in this file is visible here. If you want to expand your culinary horizons with recipes for army worms, rootworm beetles, and crickets, you'll need to visit this site yourself.

TIP SHEET

▶ **The binoculars icon next to the first menu item shown in step 6 indicates that the file is a *gopher index*. Index files contain a search field you can use to search gopher menus for items containing particular keywords.**

▶ **You can use the File, Save As command to save a document you displayed by clicking on gopher menu items, and you can print the document by clicking on the Print toolbar button.**

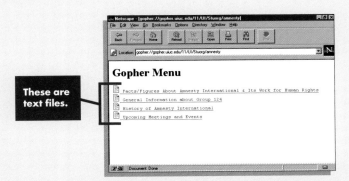

These are text files.

2 Clicking on the link displays Amnesty International's gopher server. Netscape always displays the title Gopher Menu at the top of the screen when you're displaying a directory from a gopher server. The page icons next to these four menu items indicate that they are text files.

3 The other way to connect to a gopher server is to type the URL for the site in the Location text box, and then press Enter. This URL points to Iowa State University's gopher site.

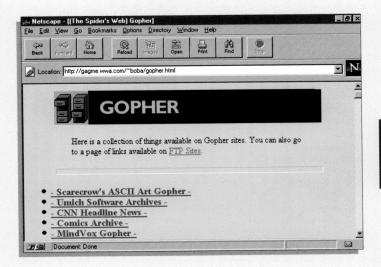

Folder icons lead to other gopher menus.

4 Netscape connects you to the top-level menu at the site. The folder icons lead to other gopher menus.

5 Clicking on the link for Colleges, Departments, and Offices displays a menu that contains a link for the Entomology Department. Click on this link to display the next menu.

6 The gopher menu for the Entomology Department contains a menu item for a text file of bug recipes.

CHAPTER 15

Safety and Security on the Internet

Not surprisingly, security is a major concern for companies and customers who want to do business on the Internet. When you send information across the Internet, there are usually at least a few points along the way where it could get intercepted. Sending a credit card number to an insecure Web site is not as risky as leaving your wallet on the dashboard of an unlocked car on a busy Manhattan street, but it's still a risk that most people are not willing to take.

To address this issue, Netscape developed a protocol called SSL (Secure Sockets Layer). SSL lets Web servers encrypt communications between you and the server so that any snoopers along the route cannot read them. This chapter begins by explaining how to recognize secure sites, and how to get detailed information about the security level of individual Web pages.

Companies who do business on the Internet typically have to keep private data and software on their internal network secure while allowing employees to access the Internet and the Web. Here, you'll learn a few strategies for protecting internal information from potential Internet intruders.

The Internet has always celebrated freedom of expression, but the fact that "anything goes" also makes many parents justifiably reluctant to let their kids wander unattended in cyberspace. This chapter looks at some ways of protecting children without censoring content on the Internet.

Finally, if you download files from the Internet, you need to be vigilant about avoiding viruses. Here, you'll find out about two anti-virus programs, and you'll get some tips for lowering the risk of getting infected.

Visiting a Secure Web Site

Although secure sites represent only a small percentage of the total number of commercial sites on the Web, the number is growing rapidly. You can already conduct a wide variety of secure business transactions over the Web, from making plane reservations to buying flowers, and soon secure sites will become much more common.

▶ **1** As you know, the URLs for Web pages on standard (insecure) servers begin with *http://*. Netscape also displays a broken key on a gray background in the lower-left corner of your screen to indicate that a page is insecure. This is the standard (insecure) home page for BeHOME, a home furnishing business that takes orders over the Web.

▶ Sites can contain *mixed-security* pages, secure pages that include insecure sections. When you request one of these pages, Netscape displays a message box to tell you that parts of the page are insecure.

▶ Netscape Navigator 3.0 can store personal certificates and site certificates (Options, Security Preferences). A *personal certificate* (also called a *digital ID*) verifies your identity to others. If you visit a secure site that requires a personal certificate (most don't) your browser will automatically send the certificate for you. If you need a personal certificate, you can get one from Verisign (http://www .verisign.com). Verisign is currently issuing certificates for free, but you can expect to pay for them in the future.

▶ A *site certificate* verifies the identity of a remote Web site to you. When you connect to a secure site, the server sends the company's site certificate to your Netscape browser, and the browser confirms that it's valid before letting you browse the secure site.

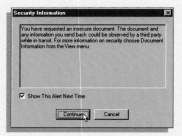

7 When you click on a link in a secure page that points to an insecure page, Netscape displays a message to let you know that a third party could observe any information you send to or receive from the requested page.

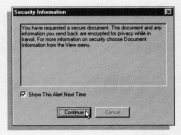

2 URLs for secure Web pages begin with *https://*. This is the URL for BeHOME's home page if you retrieve the page from BeHOME's secure server.

3 When you click on a link for a secure Web page or enter its URL in the Location text box, Netscape displays a message to let you know that any information you send or receive from the page will be encrypted. Click on the Continue button.

Blue color bar

4 Netscape now displays the secure version of BeHOME's home page. You can tell a page is secure because you see an unbroken key icon on a blue background. In addition, Netscape displays a blue color bar across the top of the content area.

6 Netscape displays the Document Info window. The top pane contains information about the structure of the page, and the lower pane contains security information. The Security line indicates the page's security level, and the Certificate information tells you who is vouching for the identity and potential security of the site. (Most companies who run a secure server obtain a site certificate from a *certifying authority* confirming the identity of the company.) Close the window when you are finished reviewing the information.

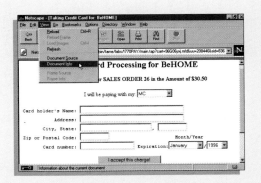

5 To find out more about the security status of a Web page, choose View, Document Info. This is BeHOME's secure page for collecting credit card information.

How Companies Maintain Security

Internet-connected companies want the advantages of global communication over the Internet, but they don't want to jeopardize their own security in the process. Most companies use some combination of the strategies discussed on this page to prevent intrusions from the Internet and to prevent sensitive information from being sent out.

▶ ❶ The most common way to protect sensitive material on a company LAN is to build a firewall. A *firewall* stands between the company's network and the Internet, creating a barrier between them.

TIP SHEET

▶ As Internet traffic increases, so does the consumption of bandwidth, which often results in slower access times. For this reason, some Internet service providers and companies who don't actually need firewalls set up Web proxies simply to take advantage of a proxy's ability to cache documents, and hence speed up access times for frequently requested documents.

▶ If your computer is behind a firewall, there may be restrictions on what parts of the Internet you can access and what kinds of things you can download.

2 Companies with firewalls set up one computer as the *proxy*. Information going to and from the Internet passes through the proxy, which evaluates it to see if it poses a security threat.

3 Proxies have another advantage: They can store Web pages frequently requested by employees in a *cache* (a temporary storage area). Proxies speed up document-access times, because in many cases the proxy can furnish a requested document from its own cache instead of retrieving the document again from the Web.

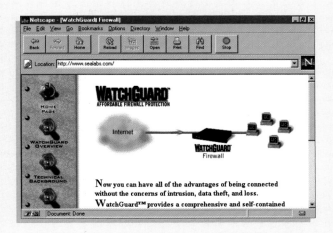

4 Another security option that many companies are turning to is the intranet. An *intranet* (or *internal Web*) is a private LAN or WAN running TCP/IP. Because intranets support HTTP, companies can set up Web sites on them just as they can on the Web at large. Many intranets have no connection to the Internet.

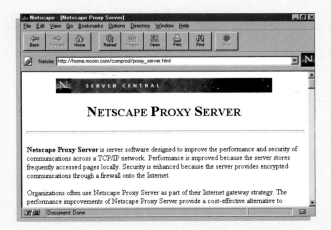

5 When companies put private corporate documents—such as company newsletters, training manuals, customer data, and product catalogs—on their intranet, employees can view them using a Web browser, but nobody outside the company can view them.

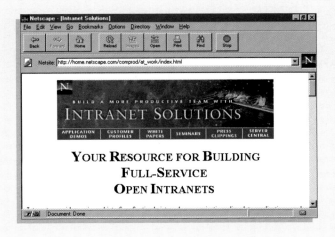

How to Keep Your Child Safe on the Web

Regardless of your views on censorship, if you're a parent and have Internet access at home, you no doubt want your children to have a positive and safe experience when they're exploring cyberspace. This page discusses three popular options: Cyber Patrol and SurfWatch are blocking programs you install on your computer, and Bess is a Web site that steers kids toward child-friendly areas of the Internet.

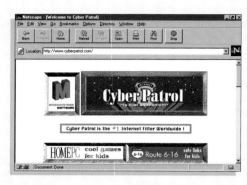

▶ **1** Cyber Patrol (http://www.cyberpatrol.com) comes with a predefined list of blocked sites (including Web sites, FTP sites, newsgroups, games, and chat facilities) called the CyberNOT list. Categories in the list include violence, drugs, intolerance, and pornography. If you wish, you can customize the CyberNOT list by unblocking particular categories or sites, or by adding specific sites to the list.

TIP SHEET

▶ **When you download Cyber Patrol, you can use the full version of the software for a week to try it out. When your time is up, you can either pay for the software or continue to use a pared-down version called the Home Edition for free. The Home Edition provides basic Internet filtering, but it doesn't let you customize the CyberNOT list, and it doesn't include most of the other features in the full version.**

▶ **Blocking programs can definitely help you monitor your child's activities on the Internet. At the same time, software can never substitute for active involvement in your child's Internet experience.**

6 When you try to access a blocked site, Bess displays the page shown here. In addition to blocking pages, Bess provides an extensive set of links to resources for children and parents on the Web.

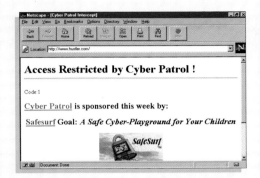

2 When you try to access a blocked site, Cyber Patrol displays the Web page shown here. Cyber Patrol includes a time-management feature that lets you specify when and for how long your child can access the Internet. And the ChatGard feature prevents your child from sending out personal information—such as name, address, or phone number—during a chat session.

3 SurfWatch (http://www.surfwatch.com) is another popular blocking and filtering program that's easy to install and simple to use.

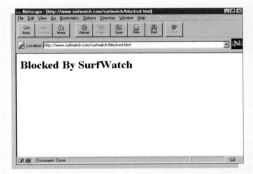

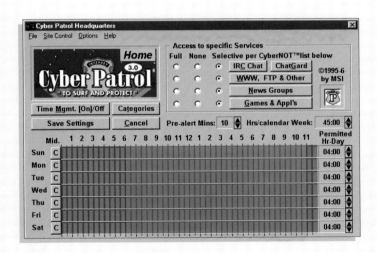

4 When you try to reach a blocked site, SurfWatch displays this page. (Notice that the page contains no ads, unlike Cyber Patrol's page!) You can customize the list of blocked sites by using a program called SurfWatch Manager, which is available for free at the SurfWatch Web site. (Starting with SurfWatch 2.0, SurfWatch Manager will be bundled into the software.)

5 Bess (http://bess.net) represents another kind of solution. To use Bess, you don't install any software on your own computer. Rather, you subscribe to the service, which then becomes your "front door" into the Internet and the Web. Bess acts as a proxy, routing all communication between your computer and the Internet through its site.

How to Protect Your Computer from Viruses

A *virus* is a program that can replicate itself and spread from one computer to the next. Once a virus makes its way onto your computer, it might lie dormant, display messages, play sounds, damage data, or crash the computer. A virus may become active anytime your computer executes an infected program. While in memory, it can do considerable damage, including replicating throughout your computer and, if you're on a network, onto other network computers. (See the Tip Sheet for a description of three most common types of viruses.) When it comes to viruses, an ounce of prevention is truly worth a pound of cure.

TIP SHEET

▶ **File viruses are usually stored in program files and spread when you load the program. You can get this type of virus by downloading and installing infected programs from the Internet, or by getting an infected program from someone on floppy disks.**

▶ **Boot-sector viruses are stored in the boot sector of a disk. When you turn on your computer, it normally reads the boot sector of your hard disk. However, if you accidentally turn on your computer while an infected floppy is still in the drive, the computer will automatically boot up from the floppy, reading the boot-sector virus into memory.**

▶ **Macro viruses are relatively new. They infect document templates, such as Word or Excel templates, and from there they spread to every document you create based on the infected template. You can get macro viruses from documents people give you on floppies or from documents you receive as e-mail attachments. (You can't get viruses by reading plain-text e-mail.)**

▶ **1** Rule #1 for warding off viruses is to only download software from reputable sites. If a site is badly organized, has broken links or out-of-date material, or looks generally sloppy, the administrator of the site may not be taking proper precautions to avoid distributing software that contains viruses.

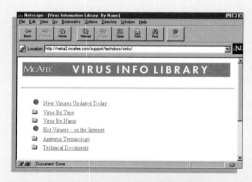

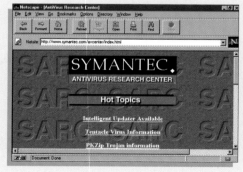

8 Both McAfee and Symantec have libraries at their Web sites that are filled with useful data, reports, and advice.

2 Because viruses are so easily spread on floppy disks, you should never (I repeat *never*) use a floppy someone hands to you without scanning it first. In particular, you should be leery of floppies your child brings home from school with the latest and greatest game. These have been popped in and out of who knows how many disk drives before ending up in your child's book bag.

3 Back up your hard disk regularly, when you know it is uninfected. If a virus causes a major crash and data gets damaged, you'll have some hope of salvaging your most important files. In the event that you have to use your backups, make sure to restore a backup you made before your computer was infected.

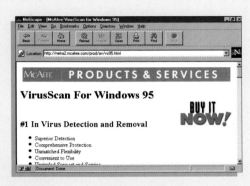

4 There are two popular anti-virus programs. One is McAfee's Virus-Scan for Windows 95 (http://www.mcafee.com).

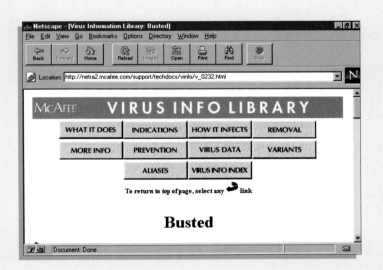

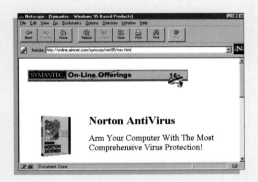

5 The other is Norton AntiVirus from Symantec (http://www.symantec.com).

7 Both Norton AntiVirus and McAfee's VirusScan load automatically when you boot up, and run in the background the entire time the computer is turned on. Anti-virus programs can help you detect viruses, clean them off your system, and repair any damage. Keep in mind, however, that this software is by necessity always one step behind the bad guys, since McAfee and Symantec can't design a fix for a virus until someone reports the virus to the company, by which time it may have already caused someone grief.

6 Symantec puts convenient monthly updates of Norton AntiVirus (which contain modifications to the program to handle newly discovered viruses) on their Web site in the form of an executable file. You can just download the file and then double-click on it to install the update.

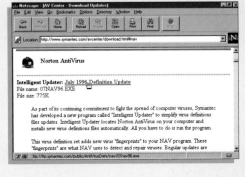

CHAPTER 16

Searching for Resources

 If traveling links randomly was the only way to find things on the Web, it wouldn't help you do much besides procrastinate from doing your real work. Fortunately, the Web offers a wide variety of search services to help you locate resources.

All the services provide *search engines* to let you hunt for Web documents by typing in keywords. Some of them also maintain more selective *directories* of Web sites that you can search by category. (One way that these services discover new sites is to use a *spider* or *robot* software that automatically travels hyperlinks on the Web to find new pages.) In addition, all the services let you search for FTP and gopher sites, newsgroup messages, and e-mail addresses as well as Web pages.

The search services discussed in this chapter—Yahoo!, Infoseek, AltaVista, and Excite—are four of the most popular ones. However, there are many others, and more are springing up every day. Search services seem by nature to be in a constant state of flux. They alter their appearance, organization, and features on almost a daily basis, so they may look a bit different than what you see here.

Netscape provides a Net Search button that gives you quick access to several search services. (If you don't see this button, choose Directory, Show Directory Buttons.) However, Netscape frequently changes the services it features. So if you like a particular service, you can bookmark the site and then jump directly to it when you want to use it.

The chapter ends with an introduction to two UNIX programs, *nslookup* and *finger*, that help you get information about people and computers on the Internet. Although these programs aren't flashy, they can really come in handy when you're trying to track down an e-mail address or find the name of a computer on the Internet.

How to Use Yahoo!

Yahoo! (http://www.yahoo.com) is one of the most well-known search services on the Web. It was founded in 1994 by two Ph.D. students at Stanford University who wanted to create a catalog of Web pages for the Stanford community. News of Yahoo! spread rapidly, and today people around the world rely on the service. Yahoo! has a team of 30 or so Web surfers who review and categorize new sites for their directory, and they also supply a search engine for searching Web documents based on keywords.

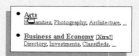

1 To search the Yahoo! directory by category, begin by clicking on one of the main categories listed in Yahoo!'s home page.

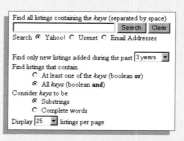

8 Yahoo! displays a relatively simple set of options for customizing your searches. You can choose the Usenet or Email Addresses option button if you want Yahoo! to search for newsgroup messages or e-mail addresses instead of Web sites. Choose the option button labeled At Least One of the Keys if you want to broaden your search to include sites containing at least one (but not necessarily all) of your keywords. Choose the Complete Words option button if you want to restrict your search results to sites that contain the exact keywords you type. (The keywords still don't have to be contiguous.)

7 By default, Yahoo! looks for Web pages whose title and contents contain *all* your 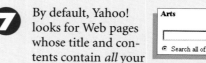 keywords. In addition, it treats keywords as *substrings* rather than complete words, looking for words that contain the keyword but may include additional characters as well. For example, in steps 5 and 6 the keyword *islam* found a site that contains the word *Islamic*. (Yahoo! searches are not case-sensitive.) If you want to change these or other search options, click on the Options link.

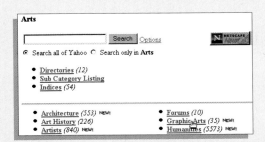

Current category

Subcategories

Sites

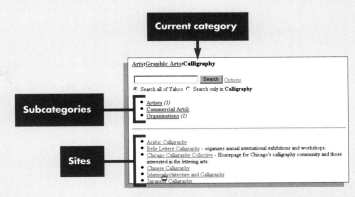

2 Yahoo displays a list of subcategories and/or sites. Continue clicking on subcategories until you see one you want to explore. If you want to go up one level, click on the Back toolbar button.

3 Click on the link for a site you want to visit. The example shown here is a link to a site about Islamic architecture and calligraphy in the Arts:Graphic Arts:Calligraphy category.

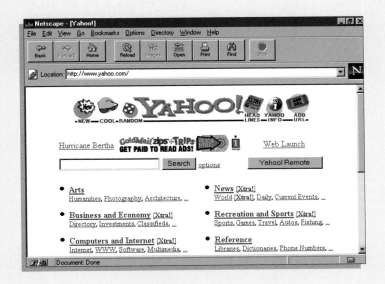

4 Netscape displays the site. If it's one you think you'll want to return to, bookmark it. To return to Yahoo!, click on the Back toolbar button.

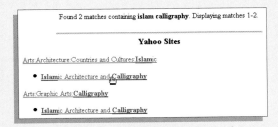

6 Yahoo! displays a list of Web pages—and the categories they belong to—that match your search criteria. In this example, the only matching Web page is the one shown in step 4 (Islamic Architecture and Calligraphy), but it happens to be cross-referenced in two separate Yahoo! categories.

5 To use the search engine, type the keywords in the Search text box (at the top of every Yahoo! directory page), choose one of the two option buttons under the text box to define the scope of the search, and click on the Search button (or press Enter). In this example, Yahoo! will search the Arts category for Web pages that contain both the words *islam* and *calligraphy*. (The keywords don't have to be adjacent to one another in the pages Yahoo! finds.)

How to Use Infoseek

Infoseek (http://www.infoseek.com) is primarily a search engine, but it also includes a directory of *Infoseek Select* sites, which the people at Infoseek have personally reviewed. To use the directory, click on the categories along the left edge of the Infoseek pages. (Because Infoseek's directory is organized just like Yahoo!, you can refer to the previous page if you need help.) This page explains how to use Infoseek's search engine and a cool feature called MapIt!

1 Infoseek assumes that you want to use its search engine to search the World Wide Web. If you instead want to search one of its directories of newsgroup messages, e-mail addresses, and so on, make the desired selection in the drop-down list under the Search for Information About text box.

8 In a minute or two, Infoseek displays a map with a red X marking the address you entered. You can change the scale of the map by clicking on the Zoom Out and Zoom In buttons. If you want to print the map, click on the Print toolbar button.

7 Infoseek displays a form entitled Find a Street Map. Type the desired address in the text boxes, and click on the MapIt! button.

Search for information about:
+house +rabbit
in the World Wide Web ▾ | seek now |

② Type your search criteria in the Search for Information About text box and click on the Seek Now button (or press Enter). In searches with more than one keyword, you can specify that a word *has* to appear in the search results by adding a plus sign directly before the word. In this example, Infoseek will look for only pages that include both the words *house* and *rabbit* (the words don't have to appear next to each other). To exclude a word from your search results, enter the word with a minus sign directly in front of it. For example, you could enter **nirvana -music** to find pages that relate to the mental state and not to the music group.

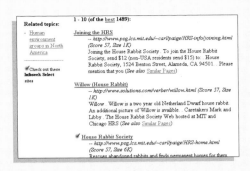

③ Infoseek displays the first page of search results. In this example, it found 1,489 Web pages that contain both the words *house* and *rabbit*. Notice that the House Rabbit Society link has a check mark icon next to it. This icon indicates that the page is listed in the Infoseek Select directory.

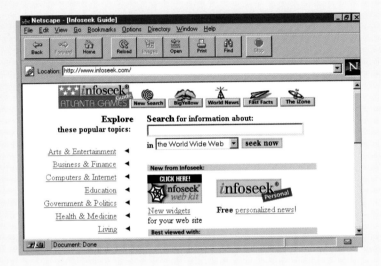

Search for information about:
[sign language learn]
in the World Wide Web ▾ | seek now |

④ If you want the keywords to be within 100 words of each other (in the same paragraph, for example), enclose them within square brackets, as shown here. If the keywords are a phrase, meaning you want them to appear in the page in that exact order, enclose them within double quotes instead of brackets.

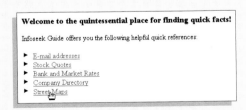

Welcome to the quintessential place for finding quick facts!

Infoseek Guide offers you the following helpful quick references:

► E-mail addresses
► Stock Quotes
► Bank and Market Rates
► Company Directory
► Street Maps

⑥ The Infoseek Web site has a program called MapIt! that generates maps on the fly for street addresses you enter. Click on Fast Facts button at the top of the Infoseek home page, and then click on Street Maps link.

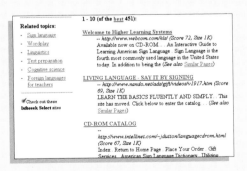

⑤ This is the first page of the search results for *[sign language learn]*. Each Web page Infoseek found contains all three keywords, but they aren't necessarily next to each other.

How to Use AltaVista

AltaVista's search engine (http://www .altavista.digital.com) indexes more pages than any other search service, and it lets you search in flexible ways. However, it doesn't offer a directory you can search by category, and the quality of the search results may be disappointing because none of the pages are reviewed. Nonetheless, the sheer volume of pages indexed by AltaVista makes it a useful service when you're searching for pages about more obscure topics.

TIP SHEET

▶ **If you want to search newsgroup articles instead of Web pages, select Usenet in the Search drop-down list (see steps 1 and 7). The Display the Results drop-down list lets you display search results in a compact form instead of the standard (detailed) form.**

▶ **Type keywords in lowercase if you want to find both lower- and uppercase instances of the word. Only use uppercase letters when you want to limit the search to words that match the combination of lower- and uppercase you type.**

▶ **If you use AltaVista frequently, you might want to make it your starting Web page when you first load Netscape. (If you don't know how to do this, refer to "How to Display Web Pages" in Chapter 5.)**

1 Type your keywords in the Search text box and click on the Submit button. To find an exact phrase, enclose the words within double quotes. In this example, AltaVista will look for Web pages containing the phrase *"Grapes of Wrath."* In searches such as this one that have multiple keywords, type a plus sign in front of a word to find only Web pages that include the word, and type a minus sign to exclude Web pages containing the word. +Steinbeck restricts the search results to pages that contain the word *Steinbeck*.

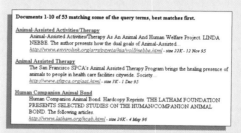

8 AltaVista displays the results. In this case, 53 pages matched the search criteria, and the pages containing the phrase *animal assisted therapy* are listed at the top.

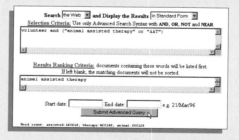

7 You can also use parentheses to group search criteria together. In this example, AltaVista will look for pages that contain the word *volunteer* and either the phrase *animal assisted therapy* or the abbreviation *AAT*. If you want Web pages that contain particular keywords to be listed first, you can type the desired keywords in the Results Ranking Criteria box. Here the pages containing the phrase *animal assisted therapy* will be listed first. To perform the search, click on the Submit Advanced Query button.

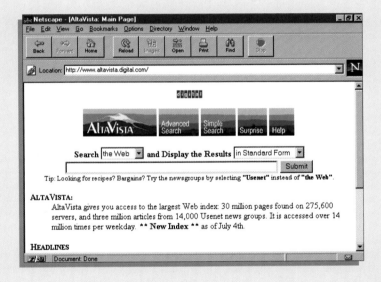

Documents 1-10 of about 500 matching some of the query terms, best matches first.

Steinbeck, John. "Grapes of Wrath". .. (ref)
　　Dr Graham Smith's Resource Information. | Linked topics | Author | Search | Edit | Utilities |
　　Steinbeck, John. "Grapes of Wrath". .. (ref) Steinbeck,...
　　http://indigo.stile.le.ac.uk/~sgi/STILE/t0000633.html - size 2K - 22 Feb 95

The Grapes of Wrath -- John Steinbeck
　　The Grapes Of Wrath Is The Book To Read. Over my educational carrer, I have read quite
　　a few books -- from picture books to short stories to long novels,..
　　http://mbhs.bergtraum.k12.ny.us/~m1127/br1.htm - size 2K - 13 Jun 96

The Grapes of Wrath by John Steinbeck
　　Historical Truth in Fiction. I have heard many stories and I have seen many films and
　　documentaries of the Great Depression. I've seen photos of the men...

2 AltaVista returns 500 matching Web pages and lists the best matches first.

3 You can use the wildcard character * in simple searches to represent one or more characters in a keyword. In this example, the keyword *organi*ational* ensures that AltaVista will include Web pages with both the British and American spellings of the word.

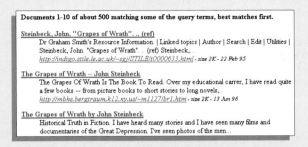

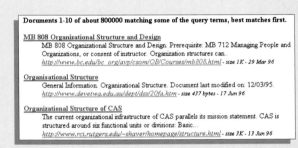

Documents 1-10 of about 800000 matching some of the query terms, best matches first.

MB 808 Organizational Structure and Design
　　MB 808 Organizational Structure and Design. Prerequisite: MB 712 Managing People and
　　Organizations, or consent of instructor. Organization structures can..
　　http://www.bc.edu/bc_org/avp/csom/OB/Courses/mb808.html - size 1K - 29 Mar 96

Organisational Structure
　　General Information. Organisational Structure. Document last modified on: 12/03/95.
　　http://www.devetwa.edu.au/dept/dss/20fa.htm - size 437 bytes - 17 Jun 96

Organizational Structure of CAS
　　The current organizational infrastructure of CAS parallels its mission statement. CAS is
　　structured around six functional units or divisions: Basic...
　　http://www.rci.rutgers.edu/~shaver/homepage/structure.html - size 3K - 13 Jun 96

4 AltaVista displays the search results. Notice that the second matching Web page uses the spelling *organisational*. (The *au* in the URL tells you that the site is in Australia.) If you had typed *z* instead of *, this Web page would not have been found.

5 If you want to perform more complex searches, click on the Advanced Search button that appears at the top of each AltaVista page.

6 Enter the search criteria in the Selection Criteria box. In an advanced search, you have to use one of the special operators: *and, or, not,* or *near.* (You can type the operators in upper- or lowercase.) Connect two keywords with *and* if you want to find only Web pages that include both words (this is the same as preceding both words with a plus sign). Connect two keywords with *or* to find Web pages containing at least one of the keywords. Precede a keyword with *not* to exclude Web pages that contain the keyword (this is the same as preceding a word with a minus sign), and connect two keywords with *near* when you want to find Web pages in which the keywords are within ten words of each other.

How to Use Excite

Excite (http://www.excite.com) includes both a directory of reviewed sites and a search engine. One of Excite's distinctive features is that by default it searches by concept instead of by the exact keywords you type. So if you type the keyword *airplane*, for example, Excite will also find Web pages about planes, jets, aircraft, or flying machines.

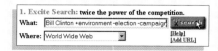

 1 Type your keywords in the What text box and click on the Search button. You can use a plus sign in front of a word in searches with multiple keywords to only find Web pages that contain the word, and you can use a minus sign to exclude Web pages containing the word. This example will look for pages about Bill Clinton and the environment that don't relate to the election campaign. (However, this will also exclude a page about a "campaign to save the environment.")

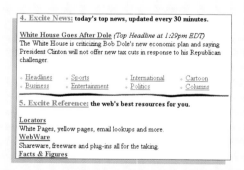

7 You can check the Excite News section of Excite's home page to find the day's top news stories, and you can use the Excite Reference section to find directory services, free software, dictionaries, maps, and more.

TIP SHEET

▶ **If you want to search newsgroup articles instead of Web sites, select Usenet Newsgroups in the Where drop-down list.**

▶ **Type keywords in lowercase if you want to find both lower- and uppercase instances of the word. Only use uppercase letters when you want to limit the search to the words that match the combination of lower- and uppercase you type.**

▶ **If you like the Excite service, you might want to make it your starting Web page when you first load Netscape. (If you don't know how to do this, refer to "How to Display Web Pages" in Chapter 5.)**

83% <u>Urge Clinton to Veto Anti-Environmental Legislation</u> [Find Similar]
URL: http://ethel.as.arizona.edu/~pathall/pastdir/950909.html
Summary: It waives the Clean Water Act and all other environmental laws, bars citizens from exercising their right to challenge illegal logging plans in court, defines salvage logging so broadly that massive clearcutting of healthy trees will be allowed, and directs the federal government to dramatically increase timber harvests. Your decision not to veto this blatantly destructive bill casts doubt...

83% <u>Archives of Action Alerts</u> [Find Similar]
URL: http://www.hwpc.org/aa1120.html
Summary: Sent 11/20/95 Last week both the House and Senate passed budget reconciliation bills which include the immediate and unconditional transfer of federal land at Ward Valley to the State of California for the construction of a nuclear dump on that site. The Ward Valley transfer provision included in the budget reconciliation bill exempts the Ward Valley nuclear dump project from all ...

2 Excite displays the results. By default, Excite sorts the Web pages it's found *by confidence,* meaning that it sorts them according to how well they match your search criteria, with the best matches at the top. To sort the results *by site* instead, click on the Sort by Site button (located at the top of the search results page).

3 Sorting by site shows you at a glance which Web pages in the results come from the same site. To go back to sorting by confidence, click on the Back toolbar button.

4 Excite lets you use the operators *and, or,* and *not.* Connect two keywords with *and* if you want to find only Web pages that include both words. (This is the same as prefacing the words with plus signs.) Use *or* to find pages containing at least one of the keywords. Precede a keyword with *not* to exclude pages that contain the keyword. (This is the same as prefacing the keyword with a minus sign.) You can also use parentheses to group search criteria together. This example will look for Web pages that relate to boats that are either canoes or kayaks.

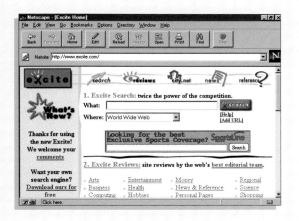

6 To use Excite's directory of reviewed sites, click on one of the main categories in the Excite Reviews section of the Excite home page. To visit sites related to a specific geographical location, choose a link in the Excite City.Net section.

5 Here are the search results sorted by site. Note that some of the pages contain the word *canoe,* and others the word *kayak.*

How to Get Information about People and Computers

Once in a while, you may need to use a UNIX program called nslookup to find an IP address or name for an Internet computer. Another UNIX program called finger can give you information about people on the Internet. There are Windows 95 versions of nslookup and finger. However, the easiest way to use these programs is to access them through Web pages designed for this purpose. (This type of page is sometimes called a gateway.) The Web pages used on this page were designed by Doug Urner, a member of the technical staff at BSDI and the technical reviewer of this book.

TIP SHEET

► **You're most likely to get a response to a finger request if the person has an Internet account at a university or a large institution with a relaxed security policy. Many companies and some ISPs block finger requests to maintain users' privacy and security at the site.**

► **Another UNIX program called *whois* lets you enter a domain name to get information about the "owners" of the domain name, including information about technical, administrative, and billing contacts. You can also enter a company name to find the company's domain name. For example, *San Francisco Online* would find sfo.com. You can access whois through another Web page designed by Doug Urner, http://www. albatross.com/whois.html.**

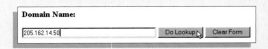

 ▶ **1** Type the URL **http://www.albatross .com/nslookup.html** and press Enter to retrieve the nslookup Web page. Type the IP address of a computer in the Domain Name text box, and click on the Do Lookup button.

8 Here are the results of the finger request. Finger gives you the login name, full name, and other information about the people currently logged onto the machine.

 7 You can omit the user name and just enter the @ symbol followed by a machine name to get information about who is currently logged onto that machine. In this example, finger will tell you who is logged into the computer named itsa.ucsf.edu.

```
nslookup results:

Server:   wobble.ALBATROSS.COM
Address:  205.230.230.1

Name:     roxy.sfo.com
Address:  205.162.14.50
```

2 Here are the results. The first two lines (for Server and Address) just list the name and IP address of the local computer that ran nslookup; the Name and Address lines contain the information you're looking for. As you can see, the name of the computer that has the IP address from step 1 is roxy.sfo.com.

3 You can also enter the name of a computer and click on Do Lookup to have nslookup return the computer's IP address.

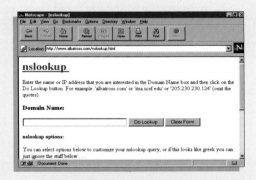

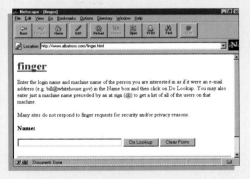

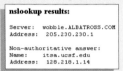

```
nslookup results:

Server:   wobble.ALBATROSS.COM
Address:  205.230.230.1

Non-authoritative answer:
Name:     itsa.ucsf.edu
Address:  128.218.1.14
```

4 nslookup tells you that the IP address for itsa.ucsf.edu is 128.218.1.14. *Non-authoritative answer* means that the name server used by wobble.albatross .com is using a cached answer to your query (someone previously looked up the IP address of itsa.ucsf.edu, and wobble.albatross.com saved the answer), so there is a slight chance that the results are no longer current.

```
results from "finger yanchen@hsc.usc.edu" at Fri Jul 12 01:09:14 PDT 1996 :

[hsc.usc.edu]
Login name: yanchen              In real life: Yan Chen
Office: DVRC 210,  HSC           Home phone: x2-6649
Directory: /home/hsc-01/yanchen  Shell: /bin/csh
Last login Thu Jul 11 13:41 on pts/82 from geeta.hsc.usc.ed
New mail received Fri Jul 12 00:51:49 1996;
   unread since Thu Jul 11 13:42:31 1996
No Plan.
```

5 Enter the URL **http://www.albatross .com/finger.html** to connect to the finger Web page. In the Name text box, type the e-mail address for the person you're interested in, and click on the Do Lookup button.

6 finger returns information about the person whose name you typed. The details you see will vary widely depending on how the person's Internet account is set up, although they usually include the person's full name and the time he or she last logged in.

TRY IT!

This Try It! lets you put into practice some of the skills discussed in the last several chapters and help out a friend at the same time. In this exercise, you'll send an e-mail message to a friend with information about a mailing list and Web page you think she or he will be interested in, along with a file from your disk. If you don't know anyone else who has a direct Internet account and uses a browser, you can send the message to yourself just for practice.

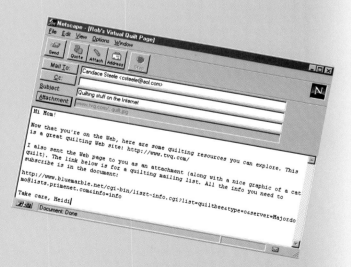

Think of a file on your disk to send your friend. If you don't already have anything appropriate, you could send a scanned photograph (most copy stores will scan photographs for you) or a long letter you write in your word processing program. (In this example, I'm going to attach a graphic image of a quilt.) Once you have decided on a file, make a mental note of which folder it's stored in.

Start Netscape. If you haven't yet used Netscape Mail, choose Options, Mail and News Preferences. (Otherwise, skip to step 4.)

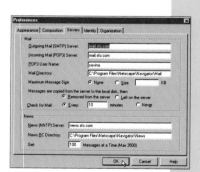

Click on the Servers tab, and make sure you've correctly filled in the Outgoing Mail (SMTP) Server, Incoming Mail (POP3) Server, and POP3 User Name text boxes. If you aren't sure, check with your ISP. (Review "Installing and Configuring Netscape" in Chapter 4 to get more help.) Then click on OK.

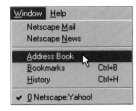

Next, you'll create an entry for your friend in Netscape's address book. (If you already have an entry for your friend, you can skip to step 7.) Start by choosing Window, Address Book.

In the Address Book window, choose Item, Add User.

In the Address Book dialog box, fill in the Nickname, Name, and E-Mail Address text boxes with the information for your friend, and optionally type a description. Then click on OK and close the Address Book window.

Now you'll use Yahoo! to search for a Web page you want to send to your friend. Type **http://www.yahoo.com** in the Location text box, and press Enter.

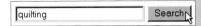

To search for sites that would interest your friend, enter a keyword or two, and click on the Search button.

Look through the results. When you find pages you might want to send to your friend, click on their links to check them out. Keep exploring until you find just the right page.

When the Web page you want to send is displayed on your screen, choose File, Mail Document.

Netscape displays the Message Composition window with the Web page's title in the subject box, the URL in the Attachment box, and a link for the site in the message area. Type the nickname for your friend in the Mail To text box (see step 6) and press the Tab key.

Continue to next page ▶

TRY IT!

Continue below

 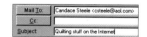

Netscape converts the nickname to the full name and e-mail address for your friend. Change the subject of the message if you like. For now, leave the rest of the message as is.

Click on Netscape's taskbar button to return to the main Netscape window, leaving the Message Composition window open.

Next, you'll use the Liszt service to find a mailing list your friend might want to join. Type **http://www.liszt.com** in the Location text box and press Enter.

Type a keyword (or two) about a subject your friend is interested in, and click on the Search button (or press Enter).

Scroll through the search results. If a link has a green [info!] icon, you can click on it to get more information about the purpose of the list. (Otherwise, just take a guess!)

Continue looking through the lists until you find one your friend might like. I displayed this information by clicking on the [info!] icon for the QuiltBee mailing list.

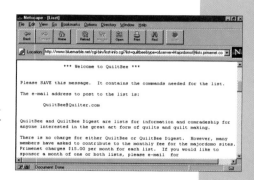

When you find a good list, right-click on either the info/information link in the description or on a green [info!] icon (both of these links contain subscription instructions) and choose Copy Link Location.

Click on the taskbar button for the Message Composition window to return to the e-mail message you started earlier in this exercise.

20

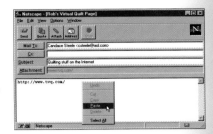

Click under-
neath the
existing URL,
right-click,
and choose
Paste from
the context menu to paste the link about
the mailing list into your message.

21

The third and
final item you'll attach to the message is
the file on your hard disk (see step 1).
Start by clicking on the Attach button
to display the Attachments dialog box.

22

The URL for the
Web site you
chose in step 10
is already listed
in the dialog box.
Click on the
Attach File button to display the Enter
File to Attach dialog box.

23

Open the
folder that
contains the
file, click on
the file name,
and click on
the Open button.

24

Leave the As Is
option button
selected, and
click on OK.

25

The file name
gets added to
the gray
Attachment
box in the
Message
Composition
window. Now type a message to your
friend. You can type text anywhere
around the two links in the message.

26

If you want to receive a copy of the
message so that you can see what your
friend will get, enter your own e-mail
address in the Cc text box.

27

Click on the
Send button to send the e-mail message along with two attachments (the
Web page and the file from your disk)
and two links (to the same Web page
and to the mailing list information).

CHAPTER 17

Getting Ready to Design a Web Site

 There are many reasons to create a Web site, not the least of which are a) you can, and b) it's fun. You can put up a Web site to let your extended family and friends know what's happening in your household, or to share expertise about a hobby or interest of yours. If you're a freelancer or consultant, you can use a Web site to tell potential customers about what you do, and show them examples of your work. If you're feeling industrious, you might want to create and run a Web site for a group you're involved with. The low cost of publishing on the Web makes it a viable option for anyone with a computer and a modem.

Read this chapter if you want to create a site, but are not sure how to begin. It will help you make some necessary decisions and gather the proper tools before starting to design your pages. First, you need to decide where your Web site will live. Once you've made this decision, you have to choose the programs you'll use to create your pages and manipulate your graphics. Finally, it doesn't hurt to learn a few principles of good Web-page design so that you can avoid some common design pitfalls.

Chapters 18 through 20 pick up where this one leaves off, teaching you how to enter and format text in a Web page, how to create hypertext links, and how to add graphics. In the Try It! after Chapter 20, you put all these skills together to create practice Web pages, and then in Chapter 21, you learn how to maintain and expand your Web site.

Obtaining Web Space

Choosing a home for your Web site isn't as important as choosing a home for yourself and your pet, but the factors you have to consider are similar. Your Web pages need to live in a space that's affordable, roomy, easy to find, and well-maintained. Most people keep their sites on an ISP's server. ISPs have the proper hardware and software, and they have a 24-hour connection to the Internet, so people browsing the Web can access your site whenever they like. This page supplies some guidelines for choosing an ISP to host your site.

▶ **①** Decide whether you want your Web site to be a part of your existing Internet account. If the site will be yours alone, it makes sense to use a single account for your Web site, for browsing the Web, and for e-mail. However, if you will be managing the Web site for an organization, you might want to keep your personal Internet account separate from the one you use for the Web site. That way, if you decide to have someone else maintain the site in the future, you won't have to change e-mail addresses.

TIP SHEET

▶ The cost of Web space varies dramatically depending on where you live. In the San Francisco Bay Area, quite a few ISPs offer 5MB to 20MB of free space with PPP accounts that cost only $20 per month, while in other areas, it's common to pay $50 to $75 per month for a PPP account and then pay extra for Web space. You might want to check with several ISPs in your area to get an idea of the price range before deciding where to house your site.

▶ To check whether a domain name is already registered to someone else, use the UNIX program whois to search for that domain name. (See the Tip Sheet in "How to Get Information about People and Computers" in Chapter 16.)

2 Think about how much space you'll need. If your pages will contain mostly text, you probably won't need more than a few megabytes of space. If, on the other hand, you want to use a lot of graphics or other multimedia files, or if you want to make software, graphics, or multimedia files available for downloading from your site, you will need much more space. To give you a rough idea of file size, most Web page graphics that fill approximately half your screen are 20 to 40K.

3 Find out if your ISP provides free Web space, and if so, how much. Some Internet accounts include no free Web space at all and some offer 20MB or more. If your ISP doesn't offer free space, find out how much extra it would cost each month to rent the space. Or check with some other ISPs, particularly if you plan on setting up a separate Internet account for the site.

4 Once you've decided where your Web site will be, make sure your ISP sends you a FAQ giving you detailed information about using your Web space. You need to know what directory on the ISP's server to place your Web pages in, and you need to know the URL for your home page.

5 If you are creating a Web site for an organization or business, you might want to get your own domain name instead of using your ISP's. Having your own domain name makes your site look well-established and makes the URL easier for people to remember. For instance, if you were planning a site for stamp collectors in San Francisco and you got a domain name of *sfstamps.com*, your URL would likely be http://www.sfstamps.com. Otherwise, your URL would be something more complicated (and more forgettable), such as http://www.ix.netcom.com/~sfstamps.

6 To get a domain name, you have to register it with an organization called InterNIC (http://www.inter-nic.net). There is a registration fee of $100 for the first two years, and an annual fee of $50 after that. Many ISPs will handle the registration process for you, although they usually charge something for the service.

Choosing an HTML Editor

You create Web pages by lacing your text with codes that are collectively called HTML (Hypertext Markup Language). These codes tell browsers how the page should be displayed. You don't have to use specialized software to write HTML; any text editor will do. However, many people like to use HTML editors because they can help you write HTML more quickly. Here, you'll learn about three options for writing HTML.

▶ **1** The low-tech (and cheap!) method of creating Web pages is to use a text editor such as Notepad. (Notepad comes with Windows 95; you can start it by clicking on the Start button, pointing to Accessories, and clicking on Notepad). You can also use your word processing program, as long as you save the file in a text-only format.

8 Hotdog's toolbars are all customizable (you can get rid of the dog bone if you don't like it), so you can easily tweak the program to suit your tastes. It has a Preview toolbar button that automatically launches your browser so you can see how your pages will look, and it includes an FTP feature to let you upload files to your Web site directly from Hotdog.

7 The most popular HTML editor at the moment is Hotdog Pro from Sausage Software (http://www.sausage.com). Unlike Netscape Editor, Hotdog does let you work with the HTML codes directly, either by typing them yourself or by inserting them with toolbar buttons or menu commands. This program comes with a zany sense of humor and enough features to create the most sophisticated of Web sites.

TIP SHEET

▶ There are many other HTML editors besides the two mentioned here. Visit the HTML Editors section of Tucows (http://www.tucows.com) if you want to try out demo versions of other programs. Most HTML editors are either freeware, or cost from $30 to $70.

▶ When you use a computer for desktop publishing, you control exactly how the finished document will appear. In contrast, when you use HTML to create a Web page, the codes only function as suggestions to browsers about how to display the page. Depending on what HTML codes the browser supports and what options the user has set in the browser, your Web page may not display as you had originally intended.

2 If you use a text editor, you have to type the HTML codes manually instead of inserting them with shortcuts such as toolbar buttons or menu commands. Some people see this as an advantage because it forces you to understand exactly how the HTML codes work; others see it as a disadvantage because typing all the codes yourself can get pretty tedious, and you're more likely to make mistakes.

3 Unlike HTML editors, which have online help, a text editor won't give you any hints if you get stuck or forget how to use a particular code. Also, text editors don't have built-in preview or FTP features. So you'll have to switch back and forth between writing and saving the pages in the text editor and then previewing them in Netscape, and you'll need to use Netscape or another FTP program to upload the files to your Web site.

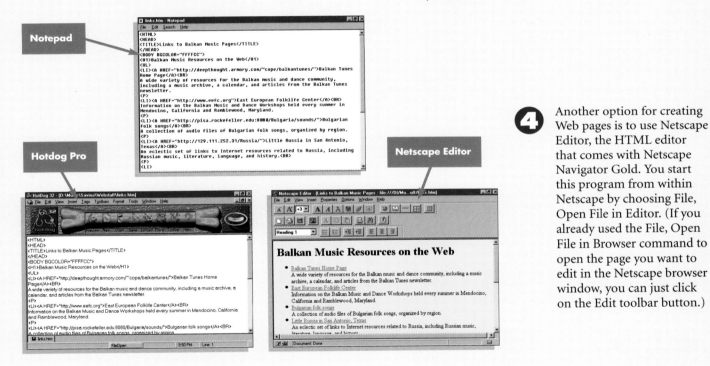

4 Another option for creating Web pages is to use Netscape Editor, the HTML editor that comes with Netscape Navigator Gold. You start this program from within Netscape by choosing File, Open File in Editor. (If you already used the File, Open File in Browser command to open the page you want to edit in the Netscape browser window, you can just click on the Edit toolbar button.)

6 One disadvantage of using Netscape Editor is that it doesn't let you type or edit the HTML codes. Rather, you write your pages by choosing toolbar buttons and menu commands, and Netscape Editor inserts the HTML codes for you in the background. While this usually works fine, it can become problematic if Netscape Editor doesn't apply the HTML codes as you had intended. To fix misplaced HTML codes, you have to specify an external HTML editor (Options, Editor Preferences), which Netscape Editor then launches when you choose the View, Edit Document Source command.

5 As you're editing a Web page in Netscape Editor, it shows you how the page will look when viewed through the browser window, although the links won't be active. If you want to test the links, simply click on the View in Browser toolbar button. Click on the Edit toolbar button in the browser window to go back to Netscape Editor.

Choosing an Image Editor

Because the Web is a graphical medium, people like to use graphics in their Web pages. Regardless of what graphic images you use—clipart, custom-designed images, photographs, and so on—you need an image editor to get them just right for your pages. Among other things, an image editor can help you resize or crop an image, add borders, or convert an image to a different file format. This page describes three shareware image editors: Lview Pro, WebImage, and Paint Shop Pro.

▶ **1** Lview Pro (http://www.lview.com) has a simple interface, but it allows you to edit the appearance of your images in a wide variety of ways. The CD-ROM version of Lview Pro also comes with over 800 images you can use in your pages.

TIP SHEET

▶ If you want to create your own graphics, you might want to explore the capabilities of Paint Shop Pro before investing in an expensive commercial graphics program such as CorelDraw!

▶ If you just want your Web page to include some text with fancy formatting (borders around the letters, shading, shadows, and so on), you might be able to use WordArt, a program for adding special effects to text that comes with Word for Windows.

2 For simple modifications—changing the size of an image or placing some text on top of it—Lview Pro should be easy for you to use. However, if you want to manipulate your image in more sophisticated ways, you might have a little difficulty understanding the menu commands, the dialog box options, and the explanations in the help system. This program seems to have been designed for experienced graphic designers who aren't afraid of math or nerdy terminology.

3 WebImage (http://www.webimage.com) is specifically designed for manipulating graphics for the Web. Consequently, many of its features are tailored to creating the types of graphics that you frequently use in Web pages, such as background images, button bars, and so on.

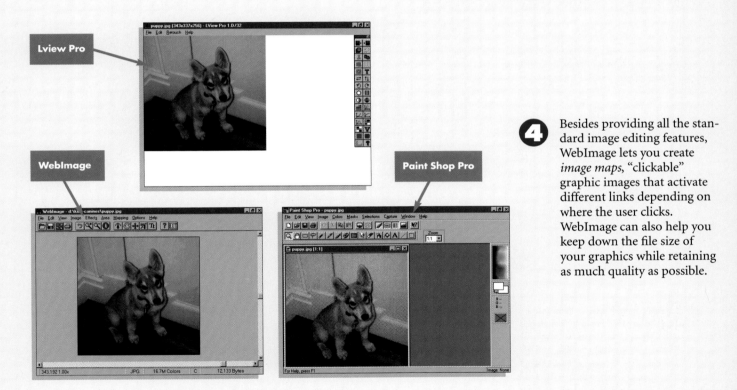

Lview Pro

WebImage

Paint Shop Pro

4 Besides providing all the standard image editing features, WebImage lets you create *image maps*, "clickable" graphic images that activate different links depending on where the user clicks. WebImage can also help you keep down the file size of your graphics while retaining as much quality as possible.

5 Paint Shop Pro (http://www.jasc.com) is more than an image editor; it is a full-fledged graphics program you can use to create, edit, and manipulate images. Unlike Lview Pro and WebImage, Paint Shop Pro comes with a full set of drawing tools for creating graphics from scratch, as well as a host of other tools for doing high-level graphic design work.

6 One other advantage of Paint Shop Pro is that it supports a huge number of file formats. This comes in handy when someone hands you a graphic image saved in an obscure format that most image editors don't recognize.

Learning the Principles of Good Design

If you've been browsing the Web for any length of time, you have probably come across certain pages that you find pleasing to the eye, and others that make you head straight for the Back button. Obviously, you'll want your own Web pages to fall into the former category and not the latter. Here are some simple guidelines for creating pages that are engaging, attractive, and easy to read. Feel free to add to or modify this list as you fine-tune your sense of design.

1 Keep your pages simple and un-cluttered, unless you're going for a high-energy, frenetic look. If your pages are as busy as the snippet shown here, your readers will need to take deep breaths and do a yoga posture or two before reading on (http://www.yogaclass.com).

TIP SHEET

▶ **You might want to test your pages with several browsers to see how they look in each one. Unfortunately, an HTML code that one browser recognizes and renders properly might be completely ignored by another. The most important browsers to test are Netscape and Internet Explorer.**

▶ **When you come across a page you either really like or really dislike, try to figure out what design elements are creating the "look" of the page, so that you can emulate or avoid them in your own pages.**

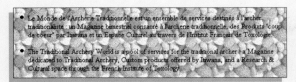

2 Make your pages easy to read. A common mistake is to use busy, colorful, and often garish backgrounds, which can make text nearly impossible to decipher. In this example, the background image is quite soft and pretty, but it still makes the text hard to read. If you place backgrounds behind text, they should be light and subtle.

3 Use reverse type—light type on a dark background—in very small doses. Reading large amounts of reverse type can cause eyestrain. For big blocks of text, it's better to use dark text on a light background.

This is a good example of a simple, well-designed page.

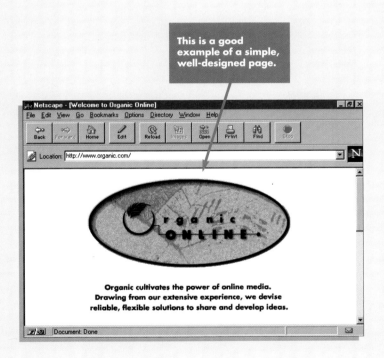

4 Use graphics judiciously. If you have too many graphics in a page or they are too large, your page will load slowly, and many people won't have the patience to wait. This map is almost 200K, and it took several long minutes to load. In this example, the sole purpose of the site is to display maps, so readers will probably be willing to wait. But graphics intended to enhance pages of text shouldn't be this large.

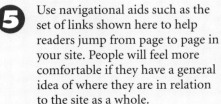

[**Advice** | **Contacts** | **Home** | **Indexes** | **Articles** | **Feedback**]

5 Use navigational aids such as the set of links shown here to help readers jump from page to page in your site. People will feel more comfortable if they have a general idea of where they are in relation to the site as a whole.

6 Consider putting a little logo at the top of each of your pages to let people see at a glance that they are still at your site.

CHAPTER 18

Entering Text in a Web Page

 HTML (Hypertext Markup Language) is called a *markup language* because you use it to mark up plain text with *tags,* which tell browsers how to format the document and what graphics and hypertext links to include. In this chapter, you learn how to construct the framework of an HTML document, and then you learn a wide variety of techniques for entering and formatting text.

HTML specifications (versions) are developed by the World Wide Web Consortium (http://www.w3.org) in cooperation with companies such as Microsoft, IBM, and Netscape. Software companies design their browsers to support as much or as little of each specification as they choose. In addition, companies can have their browsers support features that are not officially a part of HTML. As of this writing, the consortium is working on a draft of a new specification called HTML 3.2. Some browsers already support most of this new specification, but others do not.

Given this confusing and rapidly changing state of affairs, it's best to learn bread-and-butter HTML features supported by most browsers, and assume that if you use any new "bells and whistles," your pages might not display properly in some browsers. The tags discussed in this chapter and the remaining chapters of the book are, unless otherwise noted, part of HTML 2.0, the current specification. You can be fairly sure that most browsers will interpret them correctly.

To make the examples accessible regardless of the program you're using to write HTML, the sample HTML code in this and the next two chapters is shown in Notepad. (To start Notepad, click on the Start button, point to Programs, point to Accessories, and click on Notepad.)

HTML Basics

This page explains what HTML tags look like and describes the HTML tags you should enter in every Web page you create. Within the framework of these tags, which define the Web page's underlying structure, you can enter any combination of text and graphics you like.

1 HTML markup tags are enclosed within angle brackets (< >) and come in pairs. You type the starting tag at the beginning of the text you want to affect, and the ending tag at the end. These three lines of text are formatted with the tag pairs for level-1 headings (<H1> </H1>), boldface (<B> </B>), and underlining (<U> </U>). Also shown is the same HTML text as viewed through Netscape. A few HTML tags, such as the line break tag (<BR>), don't have ending tags. You'll learn how to use all of these tags later in this chapter.

TIP SHEET

- ▶ HTML is not case sensitive, although many Web designers prefer to type HTML tags in uppercase so that they stand out.

- ▶ You can customize many HTML tags by adding *attributes* to the starting tag of a tag pair. For example, you can add an attribute to the <BODY> tag to define a background color for the page. You'll learn about several common attributes later in this chapter.

- ▶ If you are writing your HTML pages in Notepad, you can preview them in Netscape by choosing File, Open File (or File, Open File in Browser if you're using Netscape Gold). Always save your pages in Notepad before previewing them in Netscape. If you make changes to a page that's already open in Netscape, save the file in Notepad, then switch to Netscape and click on the Reload toolbar button to display the revised copy of the page.

- ▶ Since your ISP is probably running the Web server on a case-sensitive UNIX machine, a good strategy is to use all lowercase file names for your HTML documents. If you then also use all lowercase file names in your links (see the next chapter), you will never have problems stemming from inconsistent case.

- ▶ Use the name *index.htm* for your "home page," the page you want to display automatically when someone jumps to your URL.

7 Many HTML editors automatically include the basic codes described here in all new HTML documents. (See Hotdog Pro's default blank document in the middle of the page.) If you're writing your Web pages in Notepad, you might want to create a document containing just these codes and use it as a jumping-off point for your new Web pages.

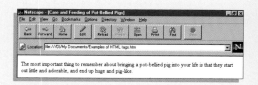

6 Line breaks and tabs you type in Notepad or any other HTML editor don't affect how the document is displayed in the browser window. For example, breaking the body text shown in step 5 into several shorter lines in Notepad has no effect on the way it appears in Netscape. You have to insert HTML tags to create separate paragraphs and adjust line breaks (see the next page). By the same token, you might want to use blank lines in your HTML editor to make the code easier to read, but they don't affect the way the page is displayed.

2 To define the structure of your Web page, begin by placing a starting <HTML> tag at the very beginning of your Web page and its ending tag </HTML> at the very end. The <HTML> tag lets browsers know that everything in the page is HTML text.

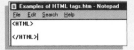

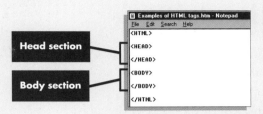

3 Within the <HTML> and </HTML> tags, Web pages are divided into two sections, head and body. The tag pair for the head section is, predictably, <HEAD> </HEAD>, and the tag pair for the body section is <BODY> </BODY>.

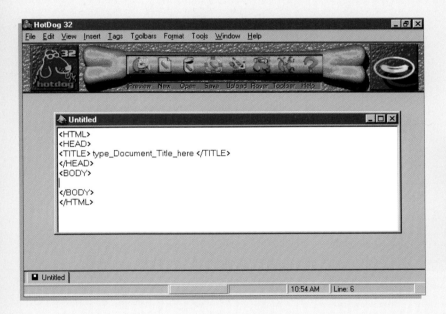

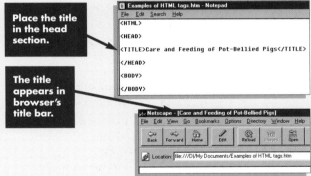

4 There are several tags you can use in the head section, but the only one that's really necessary is the <TITLE> tag. You use the <TITLE> </TITLE> tag pair to define the text that is displayed in the title bar of the browser. Titles are important because many search engines use them to index your pages.

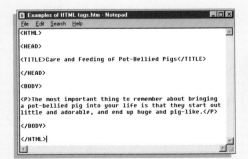

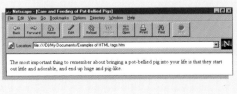

 5 You type the body of your Web page in between the <BODY> and </BODY> tags. (The <P> and </P> tags in this example are paragraph tags. You'll learn about them on the next page.)

How to Create Headings, Paragraphs, and Line Breaks

You can insert HTML heading tags to organize your Web pages into sections. You can define up to six levels of headings, although you probably won't have much need for headings lower than level 3. Within each section, you use paragraph tags to define separate paragraphs of body text, and you use line break tags to break lines within a paragraph in specific places (instead of allowing the browser to use word wrap) or to insert blank lines in the page.

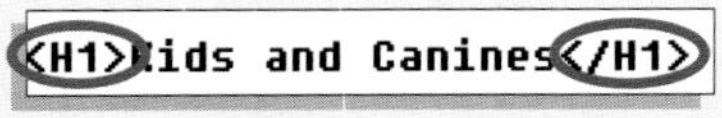

`<H1>Kids and Canines</H1>`

▶ **1** The tag pair for level-1 headings is <H1> </H1>. It's common to format the title that appears at the top of your page as a level-1 heading.

TIP SHEET

▶ All of the heading tags automatically add an extra blank line under the heading.

▶ Expect some variation in how browsers render the heading tags; even though all the popular browsers recognize the six heading levels, they may use different combinations of font size, boldface, and so on to format them.

▶ If you're using Notepad, you'll probably want to turn on the Edit, Word Wrap command so that your text wraps to fit in the Notepad window. This won't affect the line breaks in the browser.

`<H2>For kids and their tail-wagging friends</H2>`

2 You might want to use the tag pair for level-2 headings, <H2> </H2>, to format a subtitle (as shown here) or to define sub-headings under a level-1 heading. You can use the remaining tag pairs for headings (<H3> </H3> through <H6> </H6>) in the same way. Lower level headings are displayed in smaller type and with less emphatic formatting.

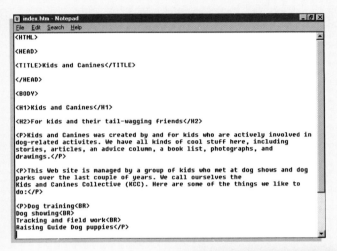

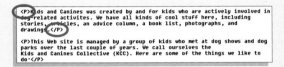

3 You use the paragraph tag pair, <P> </P>, to define separate paragraphs. Browsers automatically add a blank line above each paragraph of text defined with this tag pair. Most people omit the ending </P> tag, al-though the examples in this book include it because it may become more important in future HTML specifications.

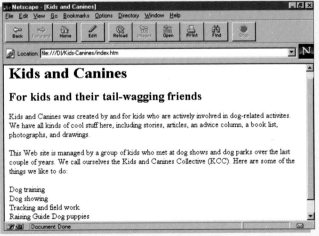

4 If you want to create several short lines of text within a paragraph, put the line break tag <BR> at the end of each line. (This tag does not have an ending tag.) Unlike the paragraph tag, the line break tag doesn't automatically add a blank line above the line containing the tag.

```
<P>Becky, Sol, Jessie, Julia, and Naishan,<BR>
<BR>
<BR>
<BR>
The Kids and Canines Collective<BR></P>
```

Becky, Sol, Jessie, Julia, and Naishan,

The Kids and Canines Collective

5 You can also use multiple <BR> tags to create several adjacent blank lines. (You can't use multiple <P> tags for this purpose.)

How to Align Headings and Paragraphs

The options for aligning headings and paragraphs are pretty basic: left (the default), center, and right. (You cannot currently specify justified alignment.) To change alignment, you add the ALIGN attribute to a heading or paragraph tag, followed by an equal sign and the desired value. You can also format paragraphs with the <BLOCKQUOTE> </BLOCKQUOTE> tag pair. Although <BLOCKQUOTE> is not technically an alignment tag, it indents the enclosed text from both the right and left, so you can use it as a convenient way to set off a block of text.

```
<H2 ALIGN=center>Kids and Canines -- Poems and Stories about Dogs</H2>
```

1 To center a heading, type **ALIGN=center** inside the starting tag. (Make sure there is a space before the word ALIGN and no spaces around the equal sign.)

```
<BLOCKQUOTE>Hi! my name is Eleah Porter. I live in Manchester, VT. I'm ten
years old. I go to Manchester Elementary Middle School. I love school a lot!
I'm in fourth grade. My teacher is Mrs. Whener. I have a dog named Norman
Spotz. He is a boy dalmatian. Norman is two years old. Norman is a lot bigger
than not His tail is very strong, it wacks me and it hurts a
lot</BLOCKQUOTE>
```

5 To indent a block of text from both sides, enclose it within the <BLOCKQUOTE> and </BLOCKQUOTE> tag pair. (Without this tag pair, the paragraph would span the full width of the browser window.)

```
<H4 ALIGN=right>Eleah Porter -- fourth grade</H4>
```

 To right-align a heading, type
ALIGN=right inside the starting tag.

```
<P ALIGN=center>Travel with me over the golden garden and hear the<BR>
daisies go daie, daie, daie, with gay.<BR>
We shall fly over beautiful skies where there's<BR>
freedom that goes ding, ding, ding, dong.<BR>
We are free, free, come, come, I am inviting you to<BR>
the land of freedom where dogs go quack, quack,<BR>
instead of bow, wow, bark, bark.<BR>
Where everything is different in mixed colors red,<BR>
yellow, pink, bluish blue.<BR>
Oh come, come to my invitation to the land of<BR>
freedom and let's be free forever. Oh diddle,<BR>
diddle dee.</P>
```

 To center all the lines of a paragraph, type
ALIGN=center inside the starting tag. You
will most likely use this option in combination with <BR> tags at the end of the lines.
Without the <BR> tags, the lines of the paragraph would automatically fill the width of
the browser window, so centering them
would have little effect.

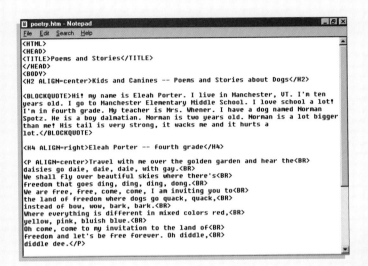

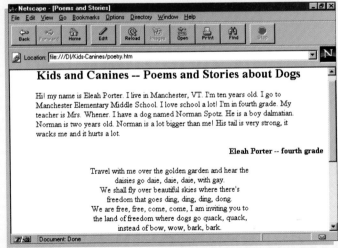

```
<P ALIGN=right>Kids and Canines Collective<BR>
1254 Orchard Street<BR>
San Anselmo, AZ 96473</P>
```

Kids and Canines Collective
1254 Orchard Street
San Anselmo, AZ 96473

 To right-align a paragraph, type **ALIGN=right** inside the
starting tag. Again, if you don't want the lines of the paragraph to word wrap automatically, use the <BR> tag to
add the desired line breaks.

How to Create Horizontal Rules

A simple way to create a visual separation between portions of your Web page is to insert a *horizontal rule*, using the <HR> tag. (This tag does not have an ending tag.) This page describes how to add horizontal rules to your documents and how to customize their appearance.

▶ ❶ To add a horizontal rule to your Web page, simply place the <HR> tag wherever you want the rule to go. (The picture in the middle of this page includes two horizontal rules.) You can modify the <HR> tag with four attributes: SIZE, WIDTH, ALIGN, and NOSHADE.

❻ If you include multiple attributes in a single tag, as shown in steps 4 and 5, you can type them in any order. For example, the tags <HR SIZE=3 WIDTH=75% ALIGN=left> and <HR WIDTH=75% ALIGN=left SIZE=3> mean the same thing to a browser.

<HR SIZE=8>

<HR SIZE=4>

2 The SIZE attribute defines the thickness of the rule, measured in pixels. The default thickness is 2 pixels; to create a thicker rule, specify a larger number of pixels. This example shows two rules, one 8 pixels wide and the other 4 pixels wide.

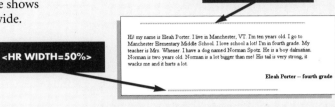

<HR WIDTH=75%>

<HR WIDTH=50%>

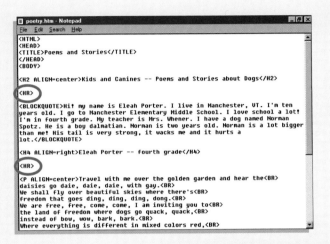

3 By default, horizontal rules extend the full width of the browser window. However, you can adjust the length of a rule with the WIDTH attribute. The easiest way to use the WIDTH attribute is to type the value as a percentage of the width of the screen. For example, <HR WIDTH=50%> creates a rule spanning only half the screen. You can also enter the WIDTH value as a number of pixels, as in <HR WIDTH=200>.

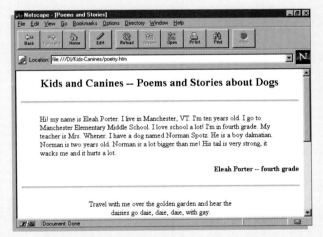

<HR ALIGN=left WIDTH=50%>

<HR ALIGN=right WIDTH=50%>

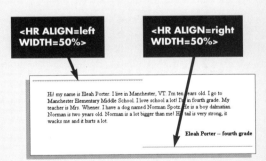

4 Horizontal rules are normally centered. If you want to left- or right-align a rule, use the ALIGN attribute. You normally use the ALIGN attribute in conjunction with the WIDTH attribute, since you wouldn't notice a change in alignment if the rule spans the full width of the window. (Separate multiple attributes with spaces.)

<HR SIZE=8 NOSHADE>

5 Use the NOSHADE attribute to remove the default 3-D shading from a rule. The effect of this attribute won't be particularly noticeable unless you increase the thickness of the rule with the SIZE attribute, as shown here.

How to Change Font Size and Appearance

If you're an experienced word processor, you probably take it for granted that you have a wide array of font-formatting options, and that you can choose among them simply by clicking on toolbar buttons. Unfortunately, HTML font formatting doesn't come close to this standard. The font-related choices in HTML are still quite limited but they are not difficult to apply.

- ▶ **If you use an HTML editor instead of Notepad, remember that toolbar buttons may let you apply font-formatting tags more quickly than you can type them "by hand."**

- ▶ **If you want, you can use the <STRONG> </STRONG> tag pair as a rough equivalent to <B> </B>. The difference is that the <STRONG> tag gives the browser more discretion in how it formats the enclosed text, although in most cases, it simply applies boldface. Along the same lines, the emphasis tag pair, <EM> </EM>, is roughly equivalent to <I> </I>.**

- ▶ **As with all other tags, you can apply multiple attributes to the <FONT> tag. For example <FONT COLOR=green SIZE=7> formats the enclosed text in a large green font.**

- ▶ **You may sometimes see a pound sign (#) before the hexadecimal value for the COLOR attribute, as in <FONT COLOR=#000080>, but you can omit the pound sign if you like.**

- ▶ **The <FONT> </FONT> tag pair is a Netscape enhancement to HTML, so it may be ignored by some browsers.**

<FONT SIZE+1> Kids and Canines Collective (KCC) </FONT>

1 To change the font size, use the SIZE attribute with the <FONT> </FONT> tag pair. You can use SIZE to specify the absolute font size or the size relative to the base font of the document. (The *base font* is the default font, unless you use the <BASEFONT> </BASEFONT> tag pair with the SIZE attribute to override the default font.) To specify an absolute size, type **SIZE=**, followed by a number from 1 to 7. The default font size is 3, so the tag <FONT SIZE=5> makes the affected text larger than normal. To specify a size relative to the base font, type SIZE=, followed by a plus or minus sign and a number. In this example, <FONT SIZE=+1> makes the enclosed text slightly bigger than the surrounding text.

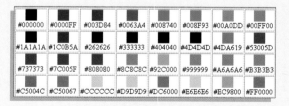

#000000	#0000FF	#003D84	#0063A4	#008740	#008F93	#00A0DD	#00FF00
#1A1A1A	#1C0B5A	#262626	#333333	#404040	#4D4D4D	#4DA619	#53005D
#737373	#7C005F	#808080	#8C8C8C	#92C000	#999999	#A6A6A6	#B3B3B3
#C5004C	#C50067	#CCCCCC	#D9D9D9	#DC6000	#E6E6E6	#EC9800	#FF0000

7 Some HTML editors let you pick colors in a dialog box, and then they convert the colors into their hexadecimal equivalents and insert the proper tags into your document. If you're taking the Luddite approach and are using Notepad, you can look on the Web for a color chart that supplies the hexadecimal numbers for the colors. Many people offer such charts as a service to Web page designers. To find one, search on a phrase such as *hex color* in Yahoo! or one of the other search services.

```
We have all kinds of <B>cool stuff</B> here
```

2 To boldface text, enclose it within the <B> </B> tag pair.

```
<I>Kids and Canines Collective (KCC)</I>
```

3 To italicize text, enclose it within the <I> </I> tag pair.

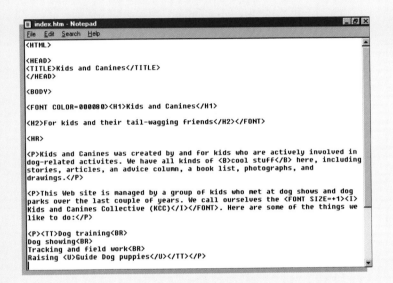

```
<HTML>

<HEAD>
<TITLE>Kids and Canines</TITLE>
</HEAD>

<BODY>

<FONT COLOR=000080><H1>Kids and Canines</H1>

<H2>For kids and their tail-wagging friends</H2></FONT>

<HR>

<P>Kids and Canines was created by and for kids who are actively involved in
dog-related activites. We have all kinds of <B>cool stuff</B> here, including
stories, articles, an advice column, a book list, photographs, and
drawings.</P>

<P>This Web site is managed by a group of kids who met at dog shows and dog
parks over the last couple of years. We call ourselves the <FONT SIZE=+1><I>
Kids and Canines Collective (KCC)</I></FONT>. Here are some of the things we
like to do:</P>

<P><TT>Dog training<BR>
Dog showing<BR>
Tracking and field work<BR>
Raising <U>Guide Dog puppies</U></TT></P>
```

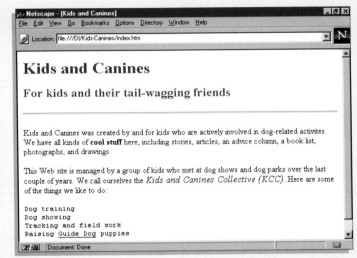

```
Raising <U>Guide Dog</U> puppies
```

4 To underline text, enclose it within the <U> </U> tag pair.

```
<FONT COLOR=000080><H1>Kids and Canines</H1>

<H2>For kids and their tail-wagging friends</H2></FONT>
```

6 To change the font color, use the COLOR attribute with the <FONT> </FONT> tag pair. You can type a color name, as in <FONT COLOR=blue>. Most browsers recognize 16 common color names, including red, blue, green, yellow, orange, magenta, pink, and brown. If you want more control over the exact color that is displayed, enter the hexadecimal notation for the color's RGB value. In this example, 000080 is hexadecimal for a dark blue. (The RGB value for a color specifies the particular percentages of red, green, and blue in that color.)

```
<P><TT>Dog training<BR>
Dog showing<BR>
Tracking and field work<BR>
Raising <U>Guide Dog puppies</U></TT></P>
```

5 You can use the typewriter-text tag pair, <TT> </TT>, to format text in a monospaced font.

How to Type Special Characters

To enter special characters such as the copyright symbol or letters in a foreign-language alphabet, you need to insert *character entities.* Character entities always begin with an ampersand (&) and end with a semicolon (;). In between these two symbols, you type the code for the particular symbol you want. Pay attention to the combination of upper- and lowercase used in the examples, because, unlike most of HTML, character entities are case sensitive. This page shows you the codes for some of the more common special characters.

```
KCC and HappyDog Bisquit&reg;</P>
<P>&copy; The Kids and Canines Collective 1997</P>
```

▶ **1** To insert the trademark registration symbol ®, type **®**. To enter the copyright symbol ©, type **©**.

`We'll post her resum&eacute; next week`

2 To enter an é, type é (or type É for an uppercase É).

`Rosario Pe&ntilde;a and her trusted assistant`

3 To insert an ñ, type ñ (or type Ñ for an uppercase Ñ).

`her trusted assistant Herr W&uuml;hfer`

4 To insert a ü, type ü (or type Ü for an uppercase Ü).

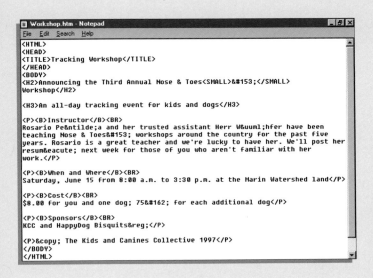

```
Workshop.htm - Notepad
File   Edit   Search   Help
<HTML>
<HEAD>
<TITLE>Tracking Workshop</TITLE>
</HEAD>
<BODY>
<H2>Announcing the Third Annual Nose & Toes<SMALL>&#153;</SMALL>
Workshop</H2>

<H3>An all-day tracking event for kids and dogs</H3>

<P><B>Instructor</B><BR>
Rosario Pe&ntilde;a and her trusted assistant Herr W&uuml;hfer have been
teaching Nose & Toes&#153; workshops around the country for the past five
years. Rosario is a great teacher and we're lucky to have her. We'll post her
resum&eacute; next week for those of you who aren't familiar with her
work.</P>

<P><B>When and Where</B><BR>
Saturday, June 15 from 8:00 a.m. to 3:30 p.m. at the Marin Watershed land</P>

<P><B>Cost</B><BR>
$8.00 For you and one dog; 75&#162; for each additional dog</P>

<P><B>Sponsors</B><BR>
KCC and HappyDog Bisquits&reg;</P>

<P>&copy; The Kids and Canines Collective 1997</P>
</BODY>
</HTML>
```

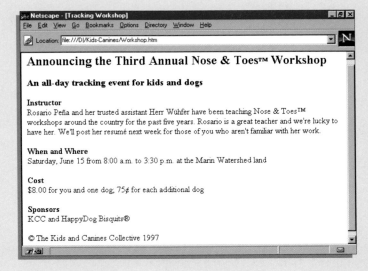

```
Netscape - [Tracking Workshop]
File   Edit   View   Go   Bookmarks   Options   Directory   Window   Help
Location: file:///D|/Kids-Canines/Workshop.htm
```

Announcing the Third Annual Nose & Toes™ Workshop

An all-day tracking event for kids and dogs

Instructor
Rosario Peña and her trusted assistant Herr Wühfer have been teaching Nose & Toes™ workshops around the country for the past five years. Rosario is a great teacher and we're lucky to have her. We'll post her resumé next week for those of you who aren't familiar with her work.

When and Where
Saturday, June 15 from 8:00 a.m. to 3:30 p.m. at the Marin Watershed land

Cost
$8.00 for you and one dog; 75¢ for each additional dog

Sponsors
KCC and HappyDog Bisquits®

© The Kids and Canines Collective 1997

`Nose & Toes&#153; workshops`

5 In addition to named character entities (like you've just seen), you can use numbered character entities to display an even broader range of characters. For example, to enter the trademark ™ symbol, you could type ™. You always type a # before the number. (You can also use the ™ character entity to insert a trademark symbol.)

`75&#162; for each additional dog`

6 Another numbered character entity that might come in handy is the one for displaying the cent symbol ¢. Type ¢ to enter this symbol.

How to Create Bulleted and Numbered Lists

HTML refers to bulleted lists as *unordered* lists, and numbered lists as *ordered* lists. Bulleted and numbered lists are extremely useful for organizing text into coherent, bite-sized pieces. Here you learn the simple steps for creating lists in your pages.

```
<UL>
</UL>
```

▶ **❶** To create a bulleted list, begin by entering the <UL> </UL> (unordered list) tag pair. You type the entire list between these two tags.

▶ **If you want blank lines between the items in your list, end each list with the <BR> tag.**

▶ **To start a numbered list with a number other than 1, use the SEQNUM attribute to the <OL> tag. To start numbering at 15, for example, you'd enter the tag <OL SEQNUM=15>.**

▶ **You can create a multilevel list if you need to list subitems within an item in your main list. When you reach an item that requires a sublist, type the item, and then on the next line, enter another <UL> or <OL> tag. Type the sublist items, using the standard <LI> tag at the beginning of each line, and end the sublist with the </UL> or </OL> tag. Then continue with the next item in the main list.**

```
1. Fill tub with warm water
2. Find dog in hiding place
3. Maneuver dog into tub
4. Wash and rinse dog
5. Stand clear for shaking
6. Give treats
```

 This is the numbered list viewed in Netscape.

```
<UL>
<LI>Dog shampoo
<LI>Several towels
<LI>Lots of treats
<LI>Even more patience
</UL>
```

 Type the items in your list, prefacing each line with the <LI> (list item) tag. This tag has an ending tag, </LI>, but you don't need to use it.

- Dog shampoo
- Several towels
- Lots of treats
- Even more patience

 Here is the list when viewed in Netscape.

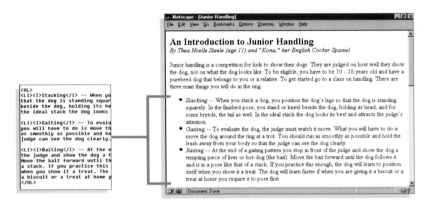

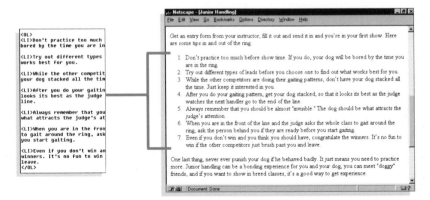

```
<OL>
<LI>Fill tub with warm water
<LI>Find dog in hiding place
<LI>Maneuver dog into tub
<LI>Wash and rinse dog
<LI>Stand clear for shaking
<LI>Give treats
</OL>
```

 Type the items in your list, prefacing each item with the <LI> (list item) tag.

```
<OL>
</OL>
```

 To create a numbered list, begin by entering the <OL> </OL> (ordered list) tag pair. As with bulleted lists, you type the entire list between these two tags.

How to Create Definition Lists

Definition lists are slightly different than bulleted and numbered lists because each item is made up of both a *term* and a *definition*. You can use a definition list for any list in which you want to include a longer indented block of text with each item in the list.

```
<DL>
</DL>
```

▶ **1** Begin by entering the <DL> </DL> (definition list) tag pair. You place the entire list inside these two tags.

```
<DL>
<DT>Newfoundland
</DL>
```

 Type the <DT> (definition term) tag and then type the first item in the list. The tag has an ending tag, </DT>, but you can omit it.

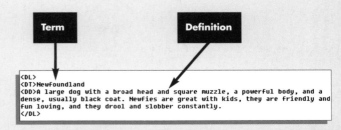

 Begin the next line with the <DD> (definition) tag, and then type the longer block of text. The ending tag for the <DD> tag, </DD>, can be omitted.

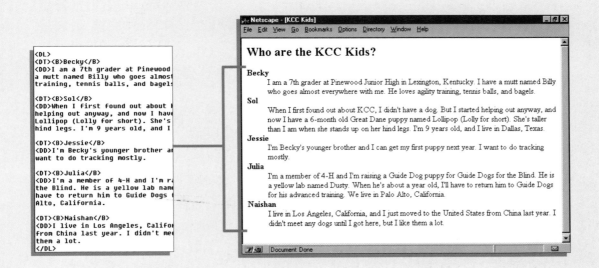

```
<DL>
<DT><B>Becky</B>
<DD>I am a 7th grader at Pinewood
a mutt named Billy who goes almost
training, tennis balls, and bagels

<DT><B>Sol</B>
<DD>When I first found out about
helping out anyway, and now I have
Lollipop (Lolly for short). She's
hind legs. I'm 9 years old, and I

<DT><B>Jessie</B>
<DD>I'm Becky's younger brother a
want to do tracking mostly.

<DT><B>Julia</B>
<DD>I'm a member of 4-H and I'm r
the Blind. He is a yellow lab nam
have to return him to Guide Dogs
Alto, California.

<DT><B>Naishan</B>
<DD>I live in Los Angeles, Califor
from China last year. I didn't me
them a lot.
</DL>
```

```
<DL>
<DT>Newfoundland
<DD>A large dog with a broad head and square muzzle, a powerful body, and a
dense, usually black coat. Newfies are great with kids, they are friendly and
fun loving, and they drool and slobber constantly.

<DT>Clumber Spaniel
<DD>A medium-size dog with short legs and a silky, predominantly white coat.
Clumber spaniels came from England and were known as the "lazy man's hunting
dog" because they tend to be on the torpid side.

<DT>Bloodhound
<DD>A large dog with a smooth coat, drooping ears, sagging jowls, and a keen
sense of smell. Bloodhounds live to sniff, so don't expect them to be
particularly social.
</DL>
```

 Repeat steps 2 and 3 until you've finished creating the list.

 Here is the list in Netscape.

CHAPTER 19

Creating the Links on a Web Page

 Creating a Web page without links would be like building a house with no front door and no doors between the rooms. Links let visitors stroll from "room to room" at your site, and "walk" from your site to others on the Web.

In this chapter, you learn how to create a number of different types of links: links to Web pages on different sites, links to other Web pages on your own site, links to other sections of the same Web page, *mailto* links, which let your visitor click on a link to send e-mail to an address you specify, and links to graphics and audio files.

Because links will be such an essential part of your site, it's a good idea to spend some time planning how you will link your pages together and what links you'll include to other sites before getting into the finer details of designing each page. Remember that the page you name *index.htm* is your "home page," the one visitors will see when they first connect to your site (assuming they don't specify a page in the URL). This page is the top level of your site, and all your other pages should cascade down from it.

Also think a bit about where you want place links to other sites. Some people prefer not to put external links on their home page because it allows people to jump in and then immediately out of the site without necessarily realizing they are leaving.

One last piece of advice: Test all your links to confirm that they're working properly before you upload your pages to your Web site. It should be *you* who finds any mistakes, not your visitors!

How to Create a Link to a Web Page at Another Site

You create all links, including those described in the rest of this chapter, by enclosing the text (or graphic) for the link within the anchor tag pair (<A> </A>). When someone views the page in a browser, this text will be underlined and displayed in a different color than the surrounding text. You then specify the target of the link by using the HREF attribute to the <A> tag. The examples in the steps come from the HTML code underlying the "Who Are the KCC Kids?" page.

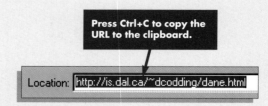

Press Ctrl+C to copy the URL to the clipboard.

Location: http://is.dal.ca/~dcodding/dane.html

▶ ❶ Part of creating a link involves entering the exact URL of the target page. Although you can do this manually—by writing down the URL and then typing it into the link—this method is tedious and you're likely to make mistakes. Here is a better strategy: Jump to the target site, select the URL in the Location text box, and press Ctrl+C to copy it to the Windows clipboard. (Now when you're ready to enter the URL in your link, you can simply paste it in.)

about KCC, I didn't ha
old Great Dane puppy
nds up off her hind legs

❺ Here is the link displayed in Netscape. When you point to the link text, the mouse pointer becomes a hand, and the target URL is displayed in the status bar. Click on the link to jump to the page. In this example, the link points to the Great Dane home page.

`6-month old <A>Great Dane</A>`

2 Open the HTML document in Notepad (or another HTML editor), and type the starting and ending anchor tags on either side of the text for the link.

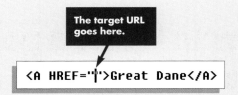

The target URL goes here.

`<A HREF="">Great Dane</A>`

3 Just to the left of the closing angle bracket in the <A> tag, type **HREF=""**, and then place your insertion point between the two double quotes, where the target URL will go.

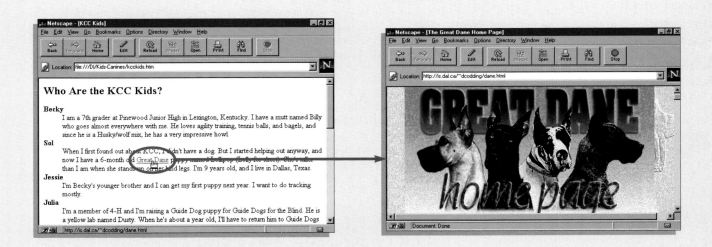

Target URL

`<A HREF="http://is.dal.ca/~dcodding/dane.html">Great Dane</A>`

4 Press Ctrl+V to paste the target URL from the Windows clipboard into the anchor tag. (Or type the URL if you didn't copy it to the clipboard as described in step 1.)

How to Create a Link to Another Page at Your Site

Before you link your own pages together, you need to decide if you want to keep all your Web documents (HTML documents and graphic files) in a single folder or in a hierarchy of folders. If you only have a few pages, it's probably easier to keep them in one folder, because that lets you list the file names without the paths in your links. If you have a lot of Web documents, you should organize them into separate folders. With this type of setup, you do have to specify the paths in your links.

TIP SHEET

▶ If you want to store your Web pages in a hierarchy of directories on your ISP's server, you should create that exact hierarchy on your hard disk and store your pages in the proper folders as you're creating them. When you're ready to go on line, you just upload the entire system of folders to the server. This ensures that all the links between your pages work.

▶ Remember to use all lowercase file names for your HTML files so that you can use all lowercase file names in your links instead of having to remember the exact combination of upper- and lowercase you used.

▶ You can use the same technique described in step 6 to link to another part of the same HTML document, as discussed on the next page.

```
<A>Kids and Canines Collective (KCC)</A>
```

▶ **1** Type the starting and ending anchor tags around the text for the link.

up of kids who met at dog shows and dog park the Kids and Canines Collective (KCC). Here

7 Here is the link as it's displayed in Netscape.

```
<A HREF="kcc/kckids.htm#jessie">
```

6 You can also link to a specific section of the target page if you've given that section a name (see the next page). To create this type of link, type the file name (and path if necessary), followed by a pound sign (#) and the name assigned to the location in the target page. In this example, the link connects to a section named *jessie* in kckids.htm, which is stored in the kcc folder.

```
<A HREF="|">Kids and Canines Collective (KCC)</A>
```

2 Type HREF="" just inside the <A> tag's closing angle bracket, and place your insertion point in between the two double quotes.

```
<A HREF="kcckids.htm">
```

3 If the target page is in the same folder as the page containing the link, you can just type the name of the target page itself. In this example, the link will connect to kcckids.htm, which is stored in the same folder (see the middle of the page).

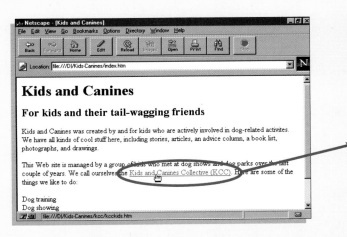

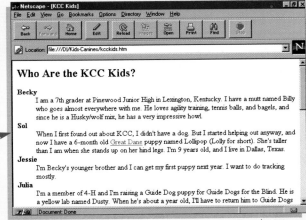

Subfolder

```
<A HREF="kcc/kcckids.htm">
```

4 If the target page is stored in a subfolder of the current folder, type the path and the file name of the page, using the forward slash (not the backslash) to separate the subfolder from the file name. (If the target page is located in a folder more than one level beneath the current folder, separate all subfolders in the path with forward slashes.)

Parent folder

```
<A HREF="../index.html">
```

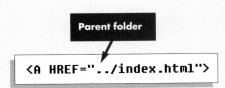

5 If the target page is stored in a folder one level up, you can use two dots (..) in the path to indicate the parent folder. In this example, the link would take the user up one level to index.html. (If the target page is in a folder more than one level above the current folder, you can use two dots for each level, separating them with forward slashes.)

How to Create a Link to Another Part of the Same Page

If your Web site includes information that visitors will probably want to print, such as a reference guide or a long article, you might want to put it on one long page instead of breaking it into smaller pages. This lets the reader print just one page instead of several. The drawback of this approach is that long pages are more awkward to move around in. One way to simplify navigation is to include links at the top of the page that point to various sections of the document.

▶ ❶ Creating links to sections of a document is a two-step procedure. First you label the sections to which you want to link, and then you add the links that point to those sections.

```
Read Thea's <A HREF="jr-handling.htm#tips">tips on
junior handling</A>.
```

❼ Remember that you can create a link in one Web page to connect to a particular section of another page, as long as you include the file name (and path if the file is in another folder) just before the #.

Includes <u>tips</u> for beginners!

❻ When readers click on the link, they will jump to the section of the document specified in the link.

TIP SHEET

▸ **Pick names for the various sections in a long document that are easy to remember. Otherwise, you'll have to double-check the names constantly as you create the links at the top of the document.**

▸ **You can use both the NAME and HREF attributes in the same <A> tag, as in <A NAME="doug" HREF="doug.jpg"> Doug's picture</A>. If you do this, the text enclosed within the starting and ending anchor tags will be the target of a link, and will itself be a link that points somewhere else.**

2 To format a block of text so that it can be the target of a link, type the anchor tags around the text. This HTML code underlies the Tips for Beginners section of the Web page entitled "An Introduction to Junior Handling."

Use the NAME attribute to label the target.

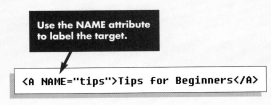

3 You use the NAME attribute with the anchor tag to label the target. Type **NAME=""** just inside the <A> tag's closing angle bracket, and type a name for the section in between the double quotes. In this example, the section is assigned the name *tips*.

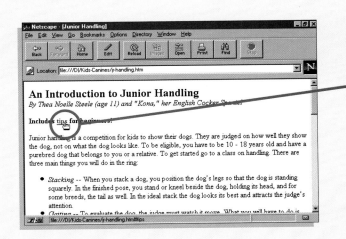

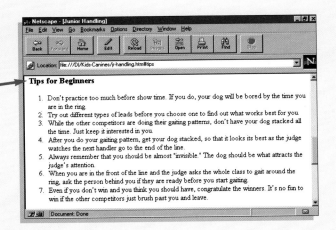

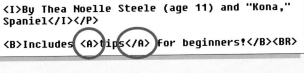

4 Next, add the <A> </A> tag pair around the text that will be the link. In this example, the link is just under the byline at the top of the document.

Use the HREF attribute to point the link to the target.

Preface the target name with #.

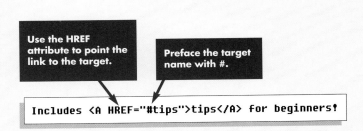

5 Type **HREF=""** just inside the <A> tag's closing angle bracket. In between the double quotes, type the name you gave the target section, prefaced with the pound symbol (#). (If you forget the #, the browser will look for an entire Web page instead of a section within a page.)

How to Create a Mailto Link

Mailto links are the easiest way to let visitors "talk" to you from your Web page. Even if you don't feel inspired to learn about incorporating interactive forms into your pages, you can still use this simple method to get comments and feedback. While it's most typical to use mailto links as a way let visitors communicate with you (the Web site administrator), you can also use them to let people send e-mail to anyone else on the Internet from your Web site.

```
By <A>Thea Noelle Steele</A> (age 11)
```

 1 Enter the anchor (<A> </A>) tag pair around the text you want to be the link.

```
<A HREF="MAILTO:">
```

2 Type **HREF="MAILTO:"** just inside the <A> tag's closing angle bracket.

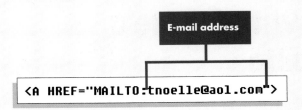

E-mail address

```
<A HREF="MAILTO:tnoelle@aol.com">
```

3 Just after the colon, type the e-mail address of the person you want the e-mail sent to. You can use your own e-mail address or anyone else's.

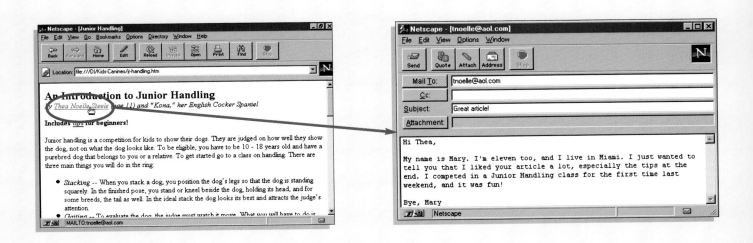

An Introduction to
By _Thea Noelle Steele_ (age 11)

4 Mailto links look just like other links; they are underlined and displayed in a different color.

5 When a visitor to your page clicks on the mailto link, his or her browser displays an e-mail window with the e-mail address you specified already entered in the Mail To text box. The visitor can then type and send the message as usual.

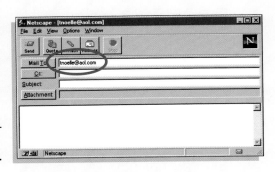

How to Create a Link to Other Graphics and Audio Files

Most of the time, you'll want to incorporate graphic images in your Web pages as *inline images* so that they display automatically. (You'll learn about inline images in the next chapter.) However, it's sometimes better to provide *links* to graphics instead. For example, if you have a large number of graphics, the page might take too long to download if you used inline images. Or a graphic might not relate that closely to the topic at hand. If you use links, readers can choose whether to view the images. By the same token, you can create links to audio files, which normally take a long time to download.

TIP SHEET

▶ You can create links to graphics or audio files on other Web sites; just include the full URL in the anchor tag.

▶ There are a variety of ways of obtaining audio files to include at your Web site. If you have a microphone and a sound card for your computer, you can make your own recordings of sound, music, or voice. There are also many archives of sounds available for downloading on the Web. (Check the Computers and Internet:Multimedia:Sound:Archives category at Yahoo!.) In addition, if you have the right sound editing software (CoolEdit is one program for Windows 95) or a professional to help you, you can extract segments of music from audio CDs and convert them to one of the standard (AU, AIFF, MIDI, or WAV) audio formats.

```
a mutt named <A>Billy</A> who
```

▶ **1** To create a link to a graphics file, first insert the <A> </A> tags around the text for the link.

```
loves agility training,
impressive howl.
```

6 When you click on the link, Netscape displays its LiveAudio window (see the middle of the page). Click on the Play button to play the file, and close the window when you are done.

```
<A HREF="billy.jpg">
```

2 Type **HREF=""** just inside the <A> tag's closing angle bracket, and type the name of the graphics file (and the path if the file is stored in another folder) in between the two double quotes. The standard file formats for graphics on the Internet are GIF and JPEG; the .jpg extension on the file shown here indicates that it's a JPEG file. (More about graphics formats in the next chapter.)

3 Now when you click on the link, Netscape displays the file in a separate window (see the middle of the page). Or if you have a helper application configured to view graphics files, Netscape launches the application for you.

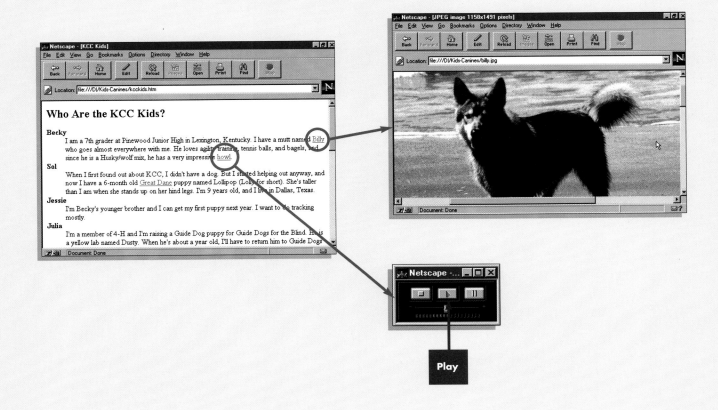

```
<A HREF="billyhowl.au">
```

5 Type **HREF=""** just inside the <A> tag's closing angle bracket, and insert the name of the audio file in between the two double quotes. Typical formats for audio files on the Internet are AU, AIFF, MIDI, and WAV.

```
very impressive <A>howl</A>.
```

4 If you want to create a link to an audio file, place the standard <A> </A> tags around the text for the link.

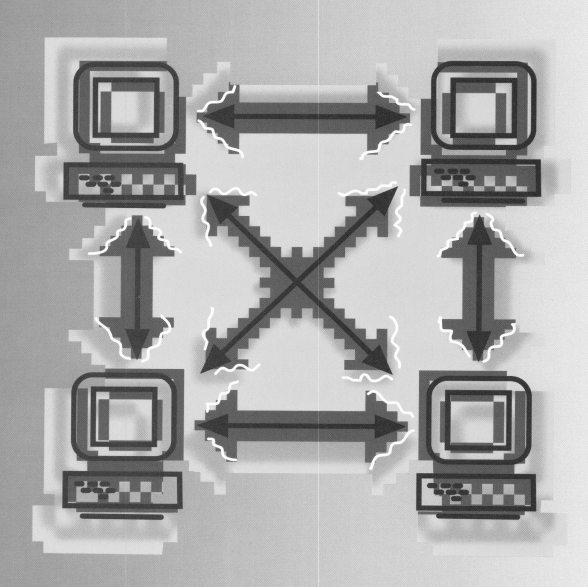

CHAPTER 20

Adding Graphics to a Web Page

 Before you actually write the HTML code to put graphics in your pages, you have to decide what images to use. One option is to use images that someone has already created. There are many archives of free images on the Web (try the Internet: Multimedia:Pictures category at Yahoo!), or some suitable clipart may have come with a word processing or graphics program you have. If you want to use photographs, you can look for ones you like in the graphics archives, or you can get your own photographs scanned at your neighborhood copy store.

The other option is to get original artwork. You can either commission a designer to create images for you (this might be expensive), or you can use a full-fledged graphics program—such as Photoshop or Paint Shop Pro—to create the artwork yourself.

Regardless of where you find your images, you'll almost certainly have to manipulate them in one way or another before you can place them in your pages. The first two topics of this chapter explain how to get your images in the right format and how to change their size.

Once you've gathered your graphics and made any necessary changes to them, you're ready to put the HTML tags into your Web pages. The last three topics in this chapter describe the HTML tags you use to place images in your pages, align them with the surrounding text, and add background colors or textures.

The examples in this chapter use Paint Shop Pro, but if you have another favorite image editor, feel free to use it instead.

How to Convert Graphic Image Formats

The two graphics formats in widespread use on the Internet are GIF (.gif) and JPEG (.jpg). These formats work well for images in Web pages because you can view them regardless of what type of computer you're using. If the image you want to use is in a format other than GIF or JPEG (BMP, PCX, WMF, and so on), you need to use an image editor to convert it one of these two formats. This page explains how to convert files and how to set a few options specific to GIF and JPEG files.

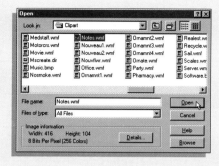

 1 To convert a file, first choose File, Open in your image editor, and then look in the Files of Type drop-down list to see if it lists the file type of your image. If it doesn't, you'll have to use a different program that can read your file. (Paint Shop Pro supports a huge number of graphics formats.) If you know your file type is supported, you can choose All Files to display all the files in the current folder. Click on the desired file, and click on Open. (The file in this example, Notes.wmf, is in Windows Metafile format, which Microsoft uses for the clipart that comes with Word for Windows.)

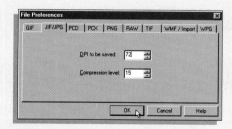

 Paint Shop Pro automatically brings the JIF/JPG tab to the front. The DPI setting controls the image resolution; the lower the number, the worse the resolution. Although 300 DPI would be appropriate for high-quality printed images, the quality of your image will be limited by the resolution of the reader's monitor. Because most monitors are 72 DPI, there isn't usually much point to setting the DPI higher than this. (A higher setting makes the file bigger and slower to download.) After you've made your changes, click on OK, and then click on Save.

- ▶ The GIF format was developed by CompuServe, although it's now used widely across the Internet.

- ▶ As a general rule, you should save images that aren't too detailed as GIF files, because GIF files are smaller than JPEGs. However, the JPEG format is better for photographs or fine drawings.

- ▶ If your image is in color, you can change the *color depth* of the image—that is, the number of colors available in the color palette for the image. If your graphic is intended for a Web page, you will probably want to reduce the color depth to 256-color (if it's currently set higher) because many monitors can't display more than 256 colors, and increased color depth means larger files. 16-color (based on the standard Windows color palette) is fine for simple graphics or icons.

- ▶ Paint Shop Pro supports the PNG format, which also allows you to create transparent images. PNG is not in widespread use on the Internet yet, although it may become more popular in the future.

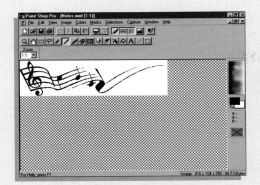

2 This opens the file in Paint Shop Pro.

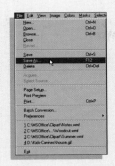

3 Choose File, Save As to display the Save As dialog box.

4 To save the file as a GIF, select GIF-CompuServe from the Save As Type drop-down list, display the Sub Type list, and choose either Version 89a-Interlaced or Version 89a-Noninterlaced. Version 87a is an older, poorer quality GIF format, and it doesn't support transparent backgrounds (see the next step). An *interlaced* GIF displays layer by layer; a *noninterlaced* GIF displays from top to bottom. Both formats take the same amount of time to download.

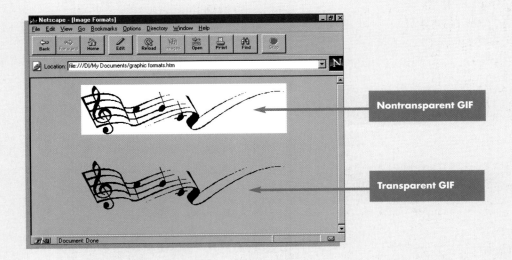

Nontransparent GIF

Transparent GIF

5 If you want to make the background color of your image transparent so that it doesn't show on the page, choose Options to display the File Preferences dialog box. (Refer to the sample transparent and nontransparent GIFs in the middle of the page.)

7 To save file as a JPEG, choose JPG-JPEG JFIF Compliant from the Save As Type drop-down list. You can leave the default Sub Type of Standard Encoding. If you want to change the DPI (dots-per-inch) setting, click on the Options button to display the File Preferences dialog box.

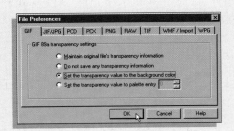

6 Paint Shop Pro automatically brings the GIF tab to the front. Choose Set the Transparency Value to the Background Color. Click on OK, and then click on the Save button.

How to Resize and Crop a Graphic Image

B ecause you will be fitting your graphic into a Web page that contains text and possibly other graphics, you'll probably need to adjust its size to make it fit just right. In addition, you might want to crop out parts of the image. Before you start experimenting with a graphic, save the file under a new name. That way, you have an original copy in case you make some changes you later regret. Most image editors also have a Revert to Saved command that reverses all changes since the last save.

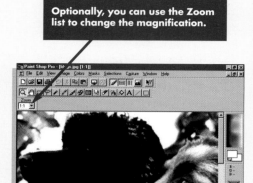

Optionally, you can use the Zoom list to change the magnification.

1 Open the image you want to resize. Paint Shop Pro displays its size (in pixels) in the lower-right corner of the screen. Keep in mind that if you have zoomed in or out (increased or decreased the magnification), the image might look larger or smaller than it really is. To display the image at its actual size, change the Zoom setting to 1:1.

> ▶ **The Zoom button (the magnifying glass) at the far left end of the tool palette is selected by default. When it's selected, you can left-click on the image to zoom in, and right-click to zoom out.**
>
> ▶ **Enlarging an image reduces its quality, whereas decreasing the size of an image actually improves its quality. For this reason, you should try to start with images that are the right size or larger than what you need in your Web page.**
>
> ▶ **Most image editors let you add borders to an image. In Paint Shop Pro, you do so by using the Image, Add Borders command.**

8 The image is cropped to the area you defined.

7 Release the mouse button, and choose Image, Crop.

2 Choose Image, and then choose Resize or Resample. The Resample command (available with JPEG files, but not GIFs) functions like the Resize command, but it uses a different calculation to resize the image. If you're resizing a photograph, the Resample command will probably do a better job of preserving image quality. With other graphics, you might want to use the Resize command because it's quicker.

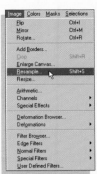

3 In the Resample (or Resize) dialog box, leave the Maintain Aspect Ratio check box selected to ensure that the image is re-sized proportionally. Type a value in pixels in the left (width) or right (height) text box, and click on OK. (As soon as you type a value, Paint Shop Pro automatically selects the Custom Size option button for you.) Because Paint Shop Pro resizes the image proportionally, you only have to fill in one of the dimensions; Paint Shop Pro calculates the other automatically.

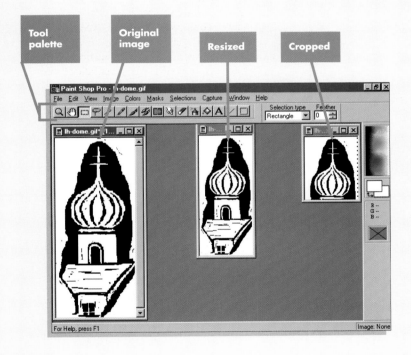

4 This is the same image reduced to a size that's suitable for a Web page.

6 Starting in the upper-left corner, drag to define the crop area.

5 To crop an image, choose the Selection button from the tool palette. In the Selection Type drop-down list, choose the shape of the selected area. (The default choice is Rectangle.) If you want, you can soften the edge of the image by increasing the value in the Feather box. (The default setting of 0 gives you the sharpest possible edge.)

How to Add a Graphic to a Web Page

You use the <IMG> tag with the SRC attribute to insert graphics into your Web pages. (The <IMG> tag doesn't have an ending tag.) The value for the SRC attribute is the name (and path if necessary) of the graphic file. If you want to turn a graphic image into a link, just enclose it within anchor tags. You can use this technique to create navigation buttons (see the image in the middle of the page) or to create thumbnail images (see the Tip Sheet).

▶ **1** Click where you want to position the graphic. Type **<IMG SRC="">**, and place the insertion point between the two double quotes.

TIP SHEET

▶ A *thumbnail* is a miniature version of an image that links to the full-size version. It's a good idea to use thumbnails if you're including a lot of graphics in your pages (in a product catalog, for example), because they'll make your pages load much more quickly. To create a thumbnail, first resize the original image to a small and manageable size; this will be your thumbnail. Then type the anchor tags around the <IMG> tag for this small-size graphic, and point to the full-size GIF or JPEG in the <A> tag's HREF attribute.

▶ All kinds of free buttons, bars (horizontal rules), icons, and more are available on the Web. A good place to start looking is the Computers and Internet:WorldWide Web:HTML:Page Layout and Design category at Yahoo!

▶ Read the next page to find out about the ALIGN=left part of the <IMG> tag for the graphic of the dog's head shown in the middle of the page.

8 Here is same graphic image with no border.

`<A HREF="doghouses.htm"><IMG SRC="dog-house.gif" BORDER=0></A>`

7 Some images have borders by default (see the doghouse image in step 6). If you want to remove a border, use the BORDER attribute with the <IMG> tag, and give it a value of 0. The value for the BORDER attribute is the border width measured in pixels. (You can also add a border to an image by specifying a value greater than 0 for the BORDER attribute, although you'll have greater control over the appearance of the border if you add it in your image editor.)

```
<IMG SRC="puppy.jpg">
```

2 Type the name of the graphic file, with the path if necessary.

```
<IMG SRC="doghead.gif" ALIGN=left>
```

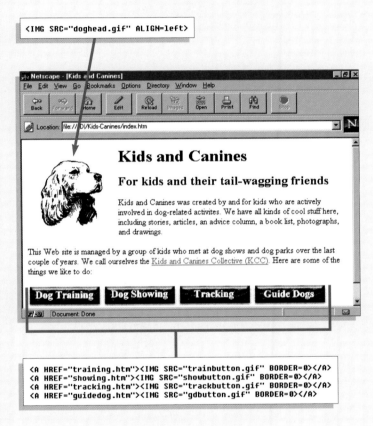

3 Here is the graphic displayed in Netscape.

```
<A HREF="training.htm"><IMG SRC="trainbutton.gif" BORDER=0></A>
<A HREF="showing.htm"><IMG SRC="showbutton.gif" BORDER=0></A>
<A HREF="tracking.htm"><IMG SRC="trackbutton.gif" BORDER=0></A>
<A HREF="guidedog.htm"><IMG SRC="gdbutton.gif" BORDER=0></A>
```

```
<IMG SRC="puppy.jpg" ALT="Photo of Sol when he was a puppy">
```

4 It's helpful to add the ALT (alternate) attribute to the <IMG> tag. The value for the ALT attribute is the descriptive text you want to display instead of the graphic if the reader is using a text-based browser or has inline graphics turned off. You must enclose the ALT text within double quotes. Starting with Navigator 3.0, Netscape automatically displays ALT text while an image is being loaded.

```
<A HREF="doghouses.htm"><IMG SRC="dog-house.gif"></A>
```

6 When you point to a graphic link in a browser window, the mouse pointer becomes a pointing hand, and when you click on the graphic, your browser displays the target of the link.

5 To turn a graphic image into a link, enclose the <IMG> tag within the <A> </A> tag pair (see Chapter 19). As usual, you use the HREF attribute to the <A> tag to specify the target of the link. This anchor tag points to a Web page named doghouses.htm.

How to Align Text Around a Graphic Image

The HTML options for controlling how text flows around a graphic image are somewhat limited. Future HTML specifications are likely to give you more flexibility in defining the layout of text and graphics on the page. In the meantime, you can experiment with the techniques described here.

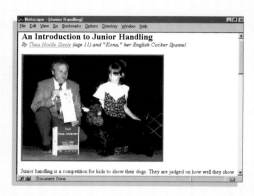

 1 By default, graphic images are displayed on the left edge of the Web page, and text is forced below the image instead of flowing around it.

TIP SHEET

▶ An attribute to the <P> tag called **CLEAR** is in the works. This tag would break the flow of text around a graphic at the point where you insert it, and force the text following the tag to move below the image. This would be much more convenient than using multiple <BR> tags. The CLEAR attribute was not yet implemented at the time of this writing, but you might check whether it has since made its way into the current HTML specification. Acceptable values for CLEAR are *left* and *right*. Use <P CLEAR=left> in situations such as the one shown in step 5, where the graphic is to the left of the text. Use <P CLEAR=right> when the graphic is to the right of the text.

▶ You can center a graphic that doesn't have surrounding text by enclosing the <IMG> tag within the <CENTER> </CENTER> tag pair. Not all browsers recognize this type of centering, however. Another option is to enclose the <IMG> attribute within the <P> </P> tag pair, and add ALIGN=center to the <P> tag.

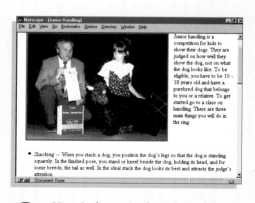

 7 Here is the revised version of the page displayed in Netscape. Notice that the bulleted list is now just beneath the photograph.

```
<IMG SRC="thea-jh.jpg" ALIGN=left HSPACE=15> <P>Junior handling
competition for kids to show their dogs. They are judged on ho
show the dog, not on what the dog looks like. To be eligible,
```

2 To make text wrap around a graphic image, you add the ALIGN attribute to the <IMG> tag. Acceptable values for horizontal alignment are *left* and *right*. In this example, ALIGN=left aligns the photograph to the left of the text. The HSPACE (horizontal space) attribute creates space between the left and right sides of the graphic image and any text that flows around it. If you don't use HSPACE, the text runs right up to the edge of the image. (The value for HSPACE is measured in pixels.)

```
<A HREF="../index.htm">
<IMG SRC="home.gif" BORDER= ALIGN=middle HSPACE=10>
Back to Home Page</A>
```

3 Acceptable values for the ALIGN attribute for vertical alignment are *middle*, *top*, and *bottom*. The default value is *bottom*, so if you don't use specify otherwise, a short line of text following a graphic will line up with the bottom edge of the image. To place short text labels in the vertical middle of buttons or icons, use ALIGN=middle. This HTML code created the button and text links shown in the next step.

The ALIGN attribute aligns the graphic in relation to the text.

The HSPACE attribute adds space between the graphic and the text.

4 The Back to Home Page link is aligned in the vertical middle of the button.

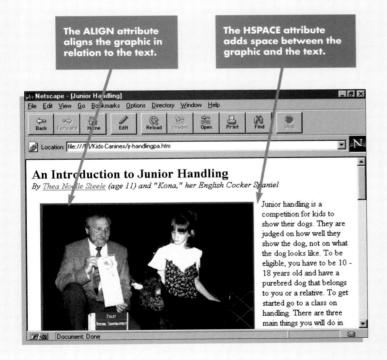

Add <BR> tags here.

5 In some situations, you need to force text below an image. In this example, it would look better if the beginning of the bulleted list (defined with the <UL> tag) began just below the photograph. To move text down below an image, add one or more
 (line break) tags.

```
10 - 18 years old and have a purebred dog t
To get started go to a class on handling. T
will do in the ring:</P>
<BR><BR><BR>
<UL>
<LI><I>Stacking</I> -- When you stack a dog
that the dog is standing squarely. In the f
beside the dog, holding its head, and for s
the ideal stack the dog looks its best and
```

6 In this example, three <BR> tags were added just above the bulleted list.

How to Add a Background Color or Texture to a Web Page

Adding a background color to a Web page can make it much more appealing visually, as long as the color is light enough that the text is still easy to read. One advantage of background colors is that they don't significantly increase the time it takes to load a page. A *texture* (sometimes called a *paper*) is a small GIF file that the browser tiles across the entire screen behind the text and graphics. Because textures consist of graphic files, they can make a page load considerably more slowly.

TIP SHEET

▶ **If you are using a background texture, you might want to boldface all the text to make it easier to read, as shown in the example in the middle of this page.**

▶ **If you want to use a transparent GIF in a Web page with a background color, use the hexadecimal notation for the color instead of the color name in the BGCOLOR attribute (for example, BGCOLOR=6AFBF0 instead of BGCOLOR=blue). Browsers may not make the background of the image transparent if the background color is not specified in hexadecimal.**

▶ **A good place to find collections of background textures is the Computers and Internet:World Wide Web:Page Design and Layout:Backgrounds category at Yahoo!**

```
<BODY BGCOLOR=6AFBF0>
```

▶ **❶** To add a background color to a Web page, you add the BGCOLOR attribute to the <BODY> tag. The value for the attribute is the hexadecimal notation for a color. (The formal syntax includes a # before the number and double quotes around it, but you can omit these elements.)

❻ In the Brightness/Contrast dialog box, decrease the contrast to a negative value. You can periodically click on the Preview button to apply the change to the image in the dialog box. When the texture looks right, click on OK and save the revised version of the file.

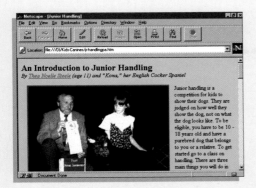

2 The hexadecimal number shown in step 1 (6AFBF0) produces a light blue color.

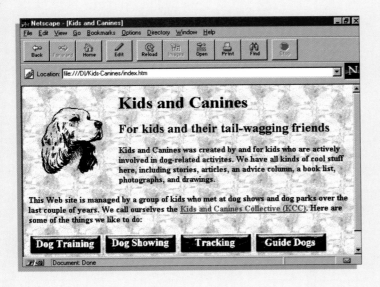

```
<BODY BACKGROUND="pnkmrbl.gif">
```

3 To add a background texture, use the BACKGROUND attribute with the <BODY> tag. The value for BACKGROUND is the file name of the GIF image. (You could use a JPEG image for a background texture, but most people use GIFs because they are smaller and load more quickly.) Enclose the file name in quotes.

4 This page shows the pnkmrbl.gif texture displayed behind a photograph.

5 It's very important that the colors in a background texture don't overpower the text. Sometimes decreasing the contrast in a texture GIF can lighten it up enough that you can use it. To adjust the contrast of an image in Paint Shop Pro, choose Colors, Adjust, Brightness/Contrast.

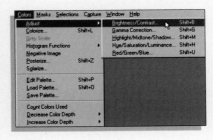

TRY IT!

This final Try It! gives you a chance to design a Web page, complete with text, a graphic image, and links. The sample page is a home page for a Web site about my neighborhood in San Francisco, but feel free to change the text, graphic image, and file names to create a page that refers to your own neighborhood! The exercise uses Notepad for the HTML editor and Paint Shop Pro for the image editor. If you're using other programs, you can still follow along—just issue the equivalent commands in your software.

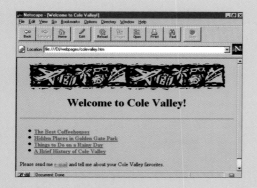

1 Start Netscape, Notepad, and your image editor. (You don't have to connect to your ISP.)

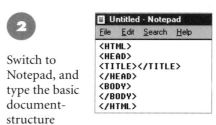

2 Switch to Notepad, and type the basic document-structure tags, as shown here.

3 Choose File, Save As, select a location for the file in the Save In drop-down list, and type a file name with an extension of .htm or .html in the File Name text box. Click on the Save button.

```
<HEAD>
<TITLE>Welcome to Cole Valley!</TITLE>
</HEAD>
```

4 Type **Welcome to Cole Valley!** between starting and ending title tags.

```
<BODY>
<H1 ALIGN=center>Welcome to Cole Valley!</H1>
</BODY>
```

5 Add the level-1 heading Welcome to Cole Valley! to the Web page, and center it with the ALIGN attribute to the <H1> tag, as shown here.

```
<HR>
</BODY>
</HTML>
```

Add a horizontal rule under the level-1 heading and just above the closing body tag.

```
<HR>
<UL>
</UL>
</BODY>
```

Type the starting and ending tags for an unordered list (<UL> </UL>).

```
<UL>
<LI>The Best Coffeehouses
<LI>Hidden Places in Golden Gate Park
<LI>Things to Do on a Rainy Day
<LI>A Brief History of Cole Valley
</UL>
```

Type the list items shown here, beginning each line with the <LI> tag. These items describe other (as yet uncreated) pages at the Web site.

```
<UL>
<LI><A HREF="coffee.htm">The Best Coffeehouses</A>
<LI><A HREF="parks.htm">Hidden Places in Golden Gate Park</A>
<LI><A HREF="rainyday.htm">Things to Do on a Rainy Day</A>
<LI><A HREF="history.htm">A Brief History of Cole Valley</A>
</UL>
```

9 Turn each list item into a link to a Web page by enclosing each item in the <A> </A> tag pair. The value for each HREF attribute is the file name of the target Web page. (You don't have to create the pages now; just make up whatever file names you like.)

10

```
<UL>
<B>
<LI><A HREF=
<LI><A HREF=
<LI><A HREF=
<LI><A HREF=
</B>
</UL>
```

Enclose the list items in the <B> </B> tag pair to boldface the list.

```
</UL>
<P>Please send me e-mail and tell me about your Cole
Valley favorites.</P>
</BODY>
</HTML>
```

11 Type the sentence shown here directly under the </UL> tag, enclosing it in the paragraph (<P> </P>) tag pair.

```
</UL>
<P>Please send me <A HREF="MAILTO:heidi@sfo.com">e-mail</A>
and tell me about your Cole Valley favorites.</P>
</BODY>
```

12 Turn the word *e-mail* into a mailto link by enclosing it in the <A> </A> tag pair and typing "MAILTO:your_e-mail_address" as the value for the HREF attribute.

13 Save the Web page again, leave the file open in Notepad, and switch to Netscape.

14

Choose File, Open File (or File, Open File in Browser if you're using Navigator Gold).

Continue to next page ▶

Continue below

 15

Display the folder that contains your Web page, click on the file name, and click on the Open button.

 16

View the partially completed Web page in Netscape. If you'd like, try pointing to the links. You'll notice that the URLs you entered in the anchor tags display in the status bar.

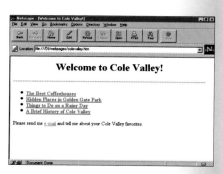

 17

Leave the Web page open in Netscape, and switch to your image editor.

 18

Open a graphic image you'd like to include in your Web page. This example uses travel.wmf, a clipart image that comes with Word for Windows 95 (Word's clipart is by default stored in the MSOffice\Clipart folder.)

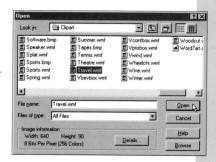

 19

Check the Zoom setting, and change it to 1:1 if necessary to view the image at its actual size.

20

Choose Image, Resize (or Image, Resample) and change the size of the image, keeping the Maintain Aspect Ratio check box marked. In this example, the width of the image is reduced from its original size of 640 pixels to 550 pixels. (Paint Shop Pro then adjusts the height accordingly.) Click on OK.

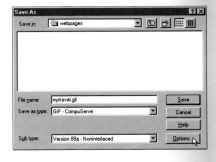

Choose File, Save As. In the Save In drop-down list, select the folder that contains your Web page, then type a new name for the graphic file in the File Name text box and select GIF - CompuServe in the Save As Type text box. Leave the Sub Type setting as is, and click the Options button if you want to make the background color transparent.

In the File Preferences dialog box, mark the option button labeled Set the Transparency Value to the Background Color, and click on OK.

Click on the Save button to save the graphic image as a GIF file. Then close the file in your image editor.

Switch back to Notepad to complete the Web page.

```
<BODY>
<IMG SRC="mytravel.gif" ALT="travel graphic">
<H1 ALIGN=center>Welcome to Cole Valley!</H1>
```

25 Add the <IMG> tag to the page directly above the level-1 heading. Use the SRC attribute to specify the graphic image you just edited, and use the ALT attribute to define the text that will display as the image is being loaded.

```
<BODY>
<P ALIGN=center><IMG SRC="mytravel.gif" ALT="travel
graphic"></P>
<H1 ALIGN=center>Welcome to Cole Valley!</H1>
```

26 Enclose the <IMG> tag in the <P> </P> tag pair, and center the paragraph by adding ALIGN=center to the <P> tag. This will center the image horizontally on the page.

```
<TITLE>Welcome to Cole Valley!</TITLE>
</HEAD>
<BODY BGCOLOR=00FFFF>
```

Add the BGCOLOR attribute to the <BODY> tag, and type the hexadecimal notation for a light color. The color shown here, 00FFFF, is a light blue-green.

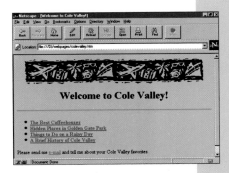

Save the file once more in Notepad, switch to Netscape, and click on the Reload button (or choose View, Reload) to load a current copy of the Web page. If you'd like, you can now create the pages referred to in the links in this page.

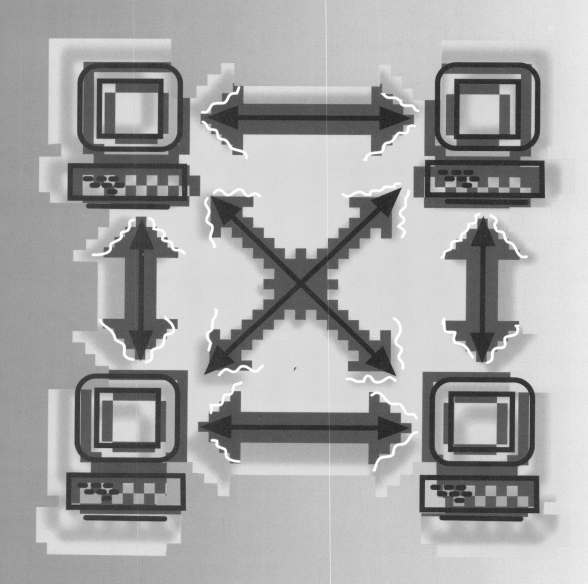

CHAPTER 21

Managing Your Web Site

 Contrary to what you might expect (or hope!), the job of running a Web site doesn't end when you finish creating a set of pages on your local hard disk. In fact, it doesn't even quite begin until you move the files up to your ISP's server to make them available to other people on the Web.

In Chapter 12, you learned how to use Netscape's FTP client to transfer individual files via FTP to a remote site. Although you could use Netscape to FTP all your Web pages and graphics one by one to your Web site, that would be a very tedious process, to say the least. A much more practical method is to use a stand-alone FTP program that lets you upload files en masse. In the first topic of this chapter, you learn how to use CuteFTP (http://www.cuteftp.com), an excellent shareware program that will make FTP transfers a breeze.

Given the decentralized nature of the Web, putting up a new Web site is a bit like opening a new stall in a crowded flea market. Few people will even know you're there unless you make a concerted effort to announce your presence. On the Web, one of the best ways to do this is to get your URL listed in the search services (see Chapter 16). The second topic in this chapter gives you some advice about this. You'll learn how to ask a service to add your site to their list, and how to design your home page so that it will be picked up by the automatic search engines.

Finally, you'll get some pointers on ways to improve your pages. Chapters 18 through 20 gave you the basic HTML skills you need to get up and running, but there are many other fun things you can do with your pages if you're looking for something to do on a rainy day.

How to Upload Files to Your Web Site

CuteFTP is a snap to use. Once you tell it how to connect to your ISP, you can simply drag multiple files or directories from your own hard disk to your ISP's computer. If there is an existing file with the same name as one you're uploading, the new file automatically overwrites the old one. You can also use CuteFTP to create directories, rename files, or delete files in your Web space. Make sure to upload any graphics or other multimedia files you're using along with the HTML pages themselves.

❶ Start CuteFTP. If CuteFTP doesn't automatically display the FTP Site Manager dialog box, click on the Site Manager toolbar button (or choose FTP, Site Manager).

The new files are uploaded.

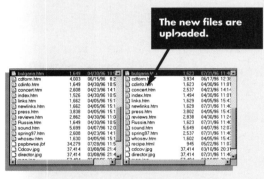

❾ A moment later, you'll see all the files you uploaded at the server.

❽ When you release the mouse button, CuteFTP displays the Confirm dialog box to ask if you want to upload the files. Click on the Yes button.

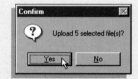

❼ To upload a group of files, select them using the usual techniques. (If the files are not adjacent, click on the first file, and then Ctrl+click on the additional files; if the files are adjacent, click on the first file, and Shift+click on the last file.) Then point to any of the selected files, and drag into the right pane. As you drag, your mouse pointer changes to show a page icon.

2 In the FTP Site Manager dialog box, click on the Personal FTP Sites category on the left side of the window, and then click on the Add Site button to display the FTP Site Edit dialog box.

3 Fill in the Site Label, Host Address, User ID, and Password text boxes. The site label is just the name CuteFTP uses in the FTP Site Manager dialog box. For the host address, you can enter either the machine name or the IP address of your ISP's computer. Optionally, you can use the Initial Remote Directory text box to specify the directory you want to display when you first connect to your ISP (probably the top-level directory of your Web space), and you can use the Initial Local Directory text box to specify the folder on your hard disk that contains most of your Web files. Leave the rest of the options as they are, and click on OK.

Site Manager

Local and remote directory buttons

Double-click on an arrow icon to move up to the parent directory.

Transfer status information

Double-click on a folder icon to move to a subdirectory.

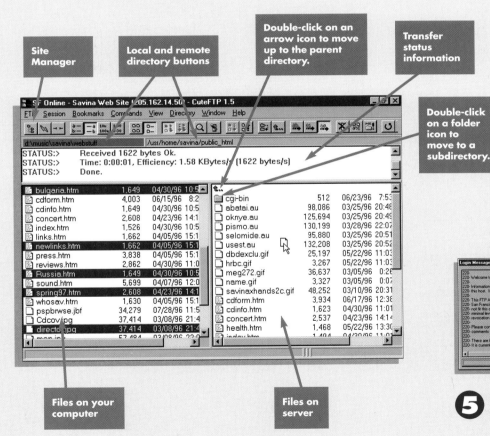

Files on your computer

Files on server

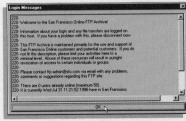

4 To connect to your Web site, click on the name in the right side of the FTP Site Manager dialog box, and then click on the Connect button.

5 If you aren't already connected to your ISP, CuteFTP displays the Connect dialog box to let you dial into your ISP's machine. As soon as you're connected, CuteFTP sends your user name and password to your ISP's FTP server. You can watch this process by keeping an eye on the top pane of the CuteFTP program window, where it displays transfer status information. If you see the Login Messages dialog box, read any new announcements, and then click on OK.

6 When you're connected to your ISP's FTP server, you see the files on your local computer on the left side of the screen and the files on your ISP's server on the right. If necessary, change directories on either or both sides. You can move up to a parent directory by double-clicking on the blue curved arrows. To move down to a subdirectory, double-click on the desired folder icon. You can also change directories on the local or remote computer by clicking on the two long gray directory buttons above the transfer status area.

How to Get Your Web Site Listed in Search Services

There are two approaches to getting your site listed in search services, and you can do both at the same time. One is to send requests to the services asking that they add your site to their index and/or directory. The other is to use tags in your HTML pages that help automatic search engines find and properly index your pages.

▶ ❶ Most search services provide a link—usually called Add Site or Add URL—that points to a form you can fill out to request that your site be added to their index. The button shown here is from Yahoo!'s home page. Alta Vista, Infoseek, Excite, and other search services have similar links.

❼ To use Submit It!, you enter information about your site into the form shown here. Submit It! then places all the information in a Web page that you can send to the various search services by clicking on buttons on the page. Not all search services accept URL submissions from Submit It!, so it's still best to use the service in conjunction with the other methods described on this page.

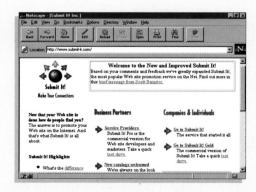

❻ You might want to take advantage of a free service on the Web called Submit It! (http://www.submit-it.com) from Scott Banister. This service automatically submits information about your site to a large number of search services.

TIP SHEET

▶ **If a page contains people's names, some search engines can index the page by those names if you enclose them in the <PERSON> </PERSON> tag pair.**

▶ **Most of the search services give helpful advice on the best way to fill out the Add URL request and on which HTML codes you should include in your pages. It's a good idea to read these instructions carefully, since every search service indexes pages differently.**

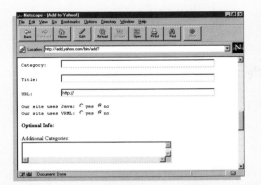

```
<TITLE>Savina Women's Folk Choir</TITLE>
```

3 There are a few things you can do with your HTML code to make sure that search engines index your page. The first is to make sure that the title of your page—the text enclosed in the <TITLE> </TITLE> tag pair—accurately describes your site (see Chapter 18). Many search engines index pages based on the title.

2 The form may only ask you for the URL, or it might ask for more detailed information, such as the name of your organization, your e-mail address, and a description of your site. This example shows the beginning of Yahoo!'s Add URL form. After you submit the form, it will probably take at least a few weeks for your form to be processed, and maybe longer if the service has a backlog of requests.

```
<IMG SRC="choir.jpg" ALT="Photograph of Savina Women's Folk Choir">
```

4 Use the ALT attribute in your <IMG> tags to describe your graphic images (see Chapter 20). Some search services use these descriptions of graphic images in their indexes.

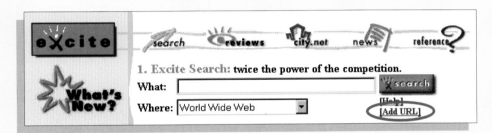

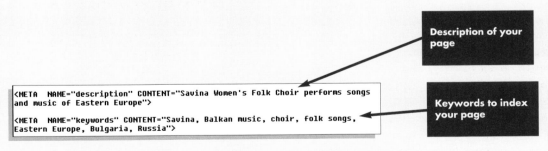

Description of your page

Keywords to index your page

```
<META NAME="description" CONTENT="Savina Women's Folk Choir performs songs
and music of Eastern Europe">

<META NAME="keywords" CONTENT="Savina, Balkan music, choir, folk songs,
Eastern Europe, Bulgaria, Russia">
```

5 Search engines such as Alta Vista and Infoseek check Web pages to look for <META> </META> tag pairs that use the NAME attribute. You can use two values with the NAME attribute: *description* and *keywords*. *Description* lets you specify the text you want to accompany your URL when it comes up in search results. *Keywords* lets you specify keywords the search engine should use to index the page. The value of the CONTENT attribute is the actual text. It's a good idea to include two <META> tags in your page, one for the description and one for keywords. Place these tags in the head section.

How to Improve Your Web Site

One of the best aspects of HTML is that you can easily view the code underlying any Web page you come across on the Web. Studying other people's code is probably one of the best ways to branch out and learn new uses of HTML. If you see a page you particularly like or a page that contains some unfamiliar design element, take a look at its HTML code to find out how it was constructed. You can then incorporate the techniques employed in that page in your own pages.

 When you find a page you want to learn from, choose View, Document Source to display the underlying HTML code. This command lets you view the source code "on the fly." If you want to study it later, you can simply save the page as an HTML file, and then open it in your HTML editor.

TIP SHEET

▶ Another great way to learn more about HTML is to read some of the online tutorials. A good place to look for them is the Computers and Internet:World Wide Web:HTML:Guides and Tutorials category of Yahoo!

▶ You can't always tell how a Web designer created every aspect of a site just by looking at the HTML code, because the code might call other programs. If this is the case, you will see the name of the program being called, but not the inner workings of the program itself. Nonetheless, you can still learn a lot about page layout and design from viewing other people's code.

▶ As you're trying new HTML features, you might want to take advantage of an HTML validation service. These services check your HTML code for syntax errors and report on what HTML specification your code conforms to. One great service is located at http://www.webtechs.com/html-val-svc. You can search for others in the Computers and Internet:Software:Data Formats:HTML:Validation/Checkers category at Yahoo!

HTML for an image map

 Here is the source code for the image map shown in step 6. Instead of typing these rather complex tags yourself, you can use one of several shareware image-mapping programs to do the hard part for you. All you have to do is trace the boundaries of each area of the graphic with your mouse, and then tell the program what URL should be linked to each part of the image. A good program to try is Web Hotspots, available at http://www.tucows.com.

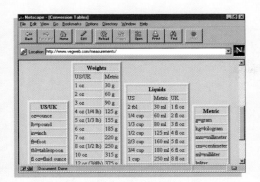

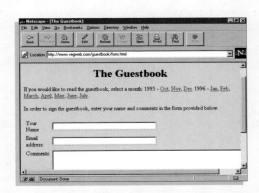

2 One HTML feature you are likely to want to learn about is tables. Tables lets you align information in rows and columns, and you can control a wide variety of formatting in the table, including the thickness of the borders, column width, row height, and so on. The four small tables shown here are typical examples of how tables can be put to good use.

3 Choosing View, Document Source displays the HTML source code for the page shown in step 2. All the code for the first of the four tables is showing on screen.

4 Another HTML feature that's rapidly becoming a standard part of Web pages is forms. You've probably filled in many forms in other people's Web pages by now, but you may want to experiment with using them to make your own pages interactive. A form then provides fields to accept input from the user, which the form then sends to some program to process. The programs called by forms in Web pages are frequently called *CGI programs*, because the Web server uses an interface called CGI (Common Gateway Interface) to pass information between the Web page and the program. People write CGI programs in a variety of programming languages, including C and Perl.

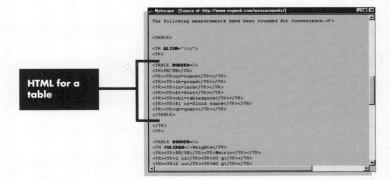

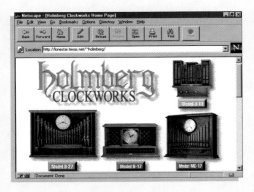

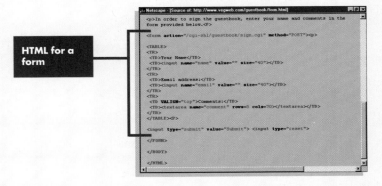

6 One other popular HTML capability you might want to explore is *image maps*. Image maps are graphic images in which different portions of the image have been "mapped" to link to different target URLs. In this example, all four clocks are part of one graphic image that the Web designer turned into an image map. Each clock points to its own separate page.

5 Here is the HTML source code for the simple guestbook form shown in step 4. The first line of the form calls a program named sign.cgi to handle the data the user types into the form.

CREDITS

I would like to thank the following individuals, whose content appears in the documents designed for this book:

Deborah Craig, photograph, page 212

Michelle Gorzycky, photograph, page 219

Lisa Hochstein, illustrations and photo retouching, pages 15, 67, 212

Anthony J. Keller and Michele Martine, photograph, page 89

Bernard W. and J. Kay Kernan, photograph, page 216

Eleah Porter, story, page 185

Rosa Rosario, poem, page 185

Edward Shoikhet, photographs, pages 171 and 207

Thea Noelle Steele, article, page 193

Doug Urner, finger and whois Web pages, page 163

INDEX